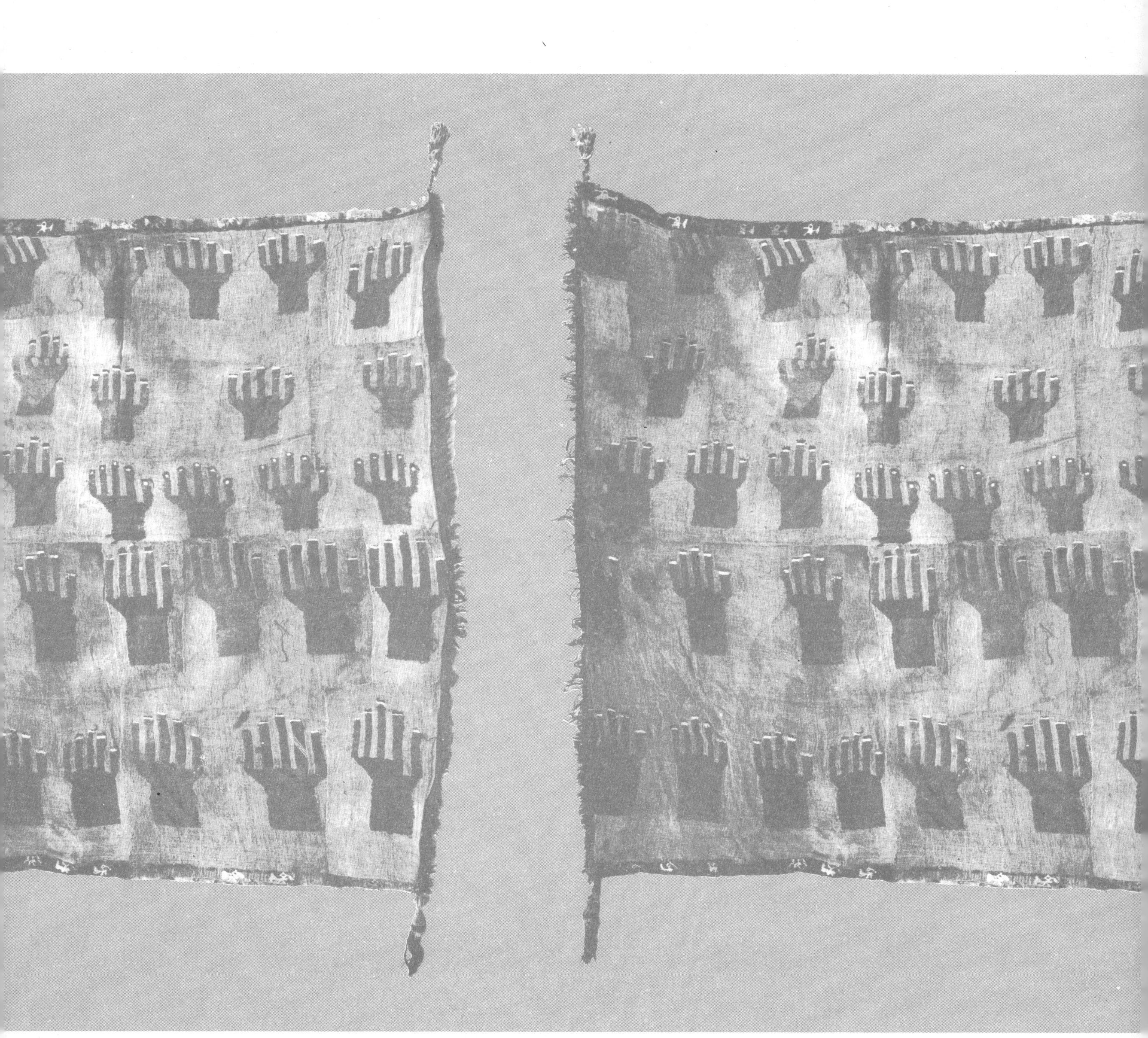

Disselhoff DAILY LIFE IN ANCIENT PERU

Hans Dietrich Disselhoff

DAILY LIFE IN ANCIENT PERU

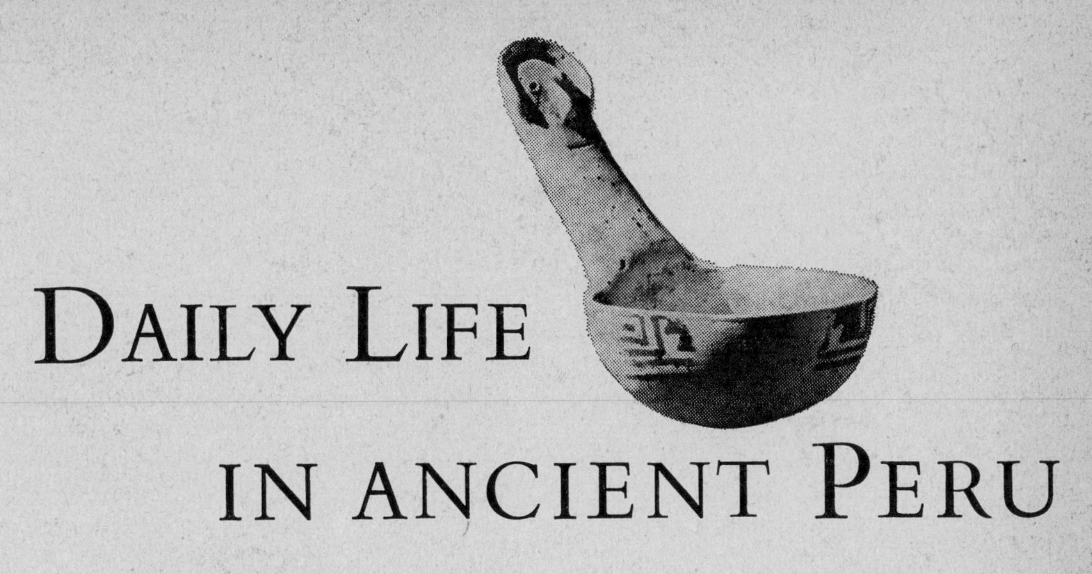

Translated from the German by Alisa Jaffa

McGRAW-HILL BOOK COMPANY

NEW YORK · LONDON · TORONTO · SYDNEY

 · Library of Congress Catalog Card No. 67-29848
17040
Printed in West Germany

Contents

Introduction

Our knowledge of Ancient America is quite recent and even today remains very incomplete. However, the barriers to our knowledge of the past are falling year by year before the archaeologist's spade. Ancient Peru, in particular, is described in a number of accounts by clergy and soldiers, who wrote of the marvels of the only true empire in America, and of its conquest. These tell how in 1532—some forty years after the discovery of the New World—Francisco Pizarro and his brothers, together with a handful of adventurers, with much courage and cunning conquered the great Indian empire. Colorful accounts of the golden land of the south do exist, dating from the 16th and 17th centuries, but such chroniclers saw this wonderland with the eyes of Europeans of their time, and for the most part with the complacency of subjects of the Catholic kings. For the Indians were not even considered human beings until a Papal decree declared them to be so.

On the 29th August 1533, the last ruling Inca, Atahualpa, was condemned to death not only for fratricide and conspiracy against the white conquerors—which was never proved—but also for polygamy and idolatry, offenses which he and his subjects did not regard as sins. In order to escape being burned at the stake, a form of execution which would have prevented the embalming of his body, thus denying him life after death, the Indian ruler allowed himself to be baptized. This motive for baptism illustrates the vast cultural gulf that lay between the captive Son of the Sun and his white executioners. After baptism, his sentence was commuted to death by strangulation, by the brutal garotte. It is reported that hundreds of Indian women killed themselves in order to accompany their dead prince to another life.

The Inca rulers appear to have possessed a kind of oral tradition, which chiefly served to extol the deified elite. So far, however, no one has been able to prove the existence of a Peruvian script akin to the picture writing and hieroglyphs of the Mexicans. There may possibly have been a whole cycle of semi-mythical oral legends relating to historical events, which formed the basis of some of the Spanish chronicles. On the whole, the 16th century chroniclers who were eye-witnesses of the conquest are more credible than the writers of later centuries, who all too often simply copied each other.

Inca history becomes more reliable with the ninth Inca, the reformer Pachacuti Yupanqui, who was crowned in 1448. When the Spanish were beginning to arrive in the country, there were still people whose fathers had been alive during the reign of this Inca—possibly the greatest of the Inca rulers. The successors of Pachacuti inherited an empire that stretched from the shores of Lake Titicaca in the High Andes to the Pacific coast, and to the Equator. They in turn extended its frontiers even farther, to the southern border of present-day Colombia in the north, and in the south as far as the River Maule which flows into the sea, south of Santiago, the Chilean capital.

This book, therefore, does not limit itself to the area contained within the modern political frontiers of Peru, nor to the short era of the Inca Empire, which lasted a bare century. The cultural history of ancient Peru (and neighboring lands) goes back thousands of years before the reign of the Incas. Ancient Peru comprised the territory governed by the Incas at the time of the Spanish landing.

We owe our knowledge and tangible evidence of Peruvian antiquity in part to archaeology and in part to the zeal of museums and private collectors in Europe and America. In earlier times even the museums used to rely almost entirely on the plunder of grave pilferers. From the beginning of the colonial period, the hunt for gold led to the looting of graves and sanctuaries. Serious archaeological research began in the earliest days of the last century. Dresden-born Max Uhle became known in Peru itself as the "father of Peruvian archaeology." He was followed by Peruvian scholars, led by Julio C. Tello, himself part-Indian, and his pupils, who developed new hypotheses about the pre-

history of their country. Thereafter archaeologists from several different European countries came to work in Peru. In the last decades, however, the most important archaeological field research has been conducted by American scholars. Peruvians, with J. Muelle at their head, have participated in every field, while the Frenchman, Frédéric Engel, has gained especial distinction for his work on the earliest pre-history of Peru.

Our subject presents us with no mean task. Since, as we have said, the Peruvians did not possess hieroglyphic writing, we have to depend on evidence made up of more brittle materials than parchment and papyrus. It consists of works of fired clay, wood, bone, metal and cotton and woolen textiles. For those who know how to interpret them, the objects found in graves provide a detailed picture of the past.

Where metals are concerned, iron was still unknown, even in the time of the Incas, and it would be more accurate to refer to a gold and copper age than to a bronze age. Unlike the Old World with its remarkable bronzes, in the region of the southern Andes bronze was not cast until approximately 1000 A.D. This costly alloy of tin and copper was used chiefly for making jewelry but also extensively for utensils, for vessels, small tweezers for plucking out hairs from body and beard, even for clubs, fish-hooks and lime spatulas for taking coca. At the very earliest gold was not worked until the last centuries before Christ. Pure copper was employed only after the birth of Christ, while stone implements and tools were still in use in the late Inca period.

In ancient Peru as in ancient Egypt, there was a great reverence for the dead and a dryness of climate. Thanks to the latter feature, such perishable materials as wood and textiles have been preserved in the desert sand of Peru. Gifts placed in graves tell of the life and nature of the Indian people over several thousands of years. This applies to a far lesser extent to the relics of the mountain dwellers, on account of the periodic rainfall in those regions. Moreover, unlike ancient Egypt, where numerous grave paintings provide visible evidence of the daily life, in ancient Peru realistic pictures painted

Drawings from left to right:

Potato harvest
Inca Pachacutic with sling, sceptre and shield
Woman weaving
Inca bridge-keeper
Inca warrior
Spanish viceroy and Inca prince

for the dead were unknown. The contents of the graves of Indian princes, too, do not compare with the riches and splendor of the tombs of the Pharaohs. From time to time the remains of frescoes are found on newly excavated temple walls. But they have always rapidly deteriorated, once they ceased to be sheltered from the open sky and were exposed to the hands of treasure seekers. Moreover, they tell us little of everyday life. For this we must turn to vase paintings, which, however, are only realistic in certain periods and certain provinces of Peru. We are dealing with peoples who, although of differing tongues, had so much in common that we may regard them as one homogeneous culture.

Even in the earliest times there was trading between the vastly differing geographical regions of the coastal strip and the mountain region. This book concerns itself with the legacies of these two main areas, without touching on the sparsely populated forestland east of the Cordillera (which was also a barrier for the Incas), since the inhabitants of this area, which constitutes by far the largest part of present-day Peru, were on a completely different level of cultural development.

More than twenty-five rivers flow down from the Andes to the desert belt of the coastal zone. Sometimes, during the dry season, they dry up almost completely, even in the mountains, but in some years during the rainy season they swell to such an extent that they cause much damage. Like little Niles, they transform the desert around their banks into green and fertile land. In ancient as in modern times, the guiding hand of man made gardens and meadows of the desert, once it was moistened by water. Nourished by the life-giving floods, shoots planted in the dusty earth turn green, producing tubers and seeds.

In the dimmest past, unknown to history, the ancestors of later farmers and planters hunted the Andean deer and small game in the bush by the lower reaches of the rivers, and caught water fowl in the marshy reed banks. Groups of fishermen caught seals and sea-lions along the shores of the Pacific, and found the occasional stranded whale, which they would cut up with their stone knives. The cold ocean current from the south that bathes the coastline is rich in fish, both large and small. The lower courses of the rivers swarm with crabs. The men would dive in among the rocks for clams and would spear sea-urchins as a special delicacy. In addition to shell-fish, the women and children gathered wild fruit and seeds. In many places along the Peruvian coast, mounds of mussel-shells can be found, remnants of the staple diet of an early fishing population.

Many peoples came and went before the food-gatherers, fishermen and huntsmen became planters and finally cultivators and gardeners, who were able to exploit the irrigated land to the full. On their arrival in Peru, the Spaniards found magnificent irrigation systems in use. Stretches of land were blooming like gardens in areas which have since ceased to be cultivated and have now reverted to desert. Aqueducts ingeniously positioned on the mountain slopes of the coastland and wide canals in the desert sand are evidence of ancient splendor. The winding courses of irrigation ditches, dried up for centuries, occasionally appear among the shifting sand-dunes.

Traces of early cultivation can be found in the deposits of refuse in the coastal region, containing remnants of food, together with fish-hooks made of mussel shells and cactus needles, stone weights for fishing nets and floats made from gourds. According to the most recent finds, some of these date back more than four thousand years before the birth of Christ. However, the cultivation of crops probably began in sheltered mountain valleys, where a great number of products were being raised in the time of the Incas (15th—16th century), which at that time were unknown to European agriculture. It was here, too, that the first agricultural terraces were built with great effort, the so-called "Andenes," from which the Andeans take their name.

Not until well after larger population groups had become settled in order to cultivate the soil did pottery appear, beginning with unadorned and badly fired shards. Before that, food had been roasted on heated stones, and cooked in gourd containers. Beans and gourds, as well as chili peppers, were among the first agricultural crops; then came tropical bulbed plants, and very much later, maize, the chief form of corn of the Mexican Indians. The vital potato was certainly first raised in the mountain areas, where an enormous variety of wild species still grow today. Cotton was an early product in the coastal region, augmenting cactus fibers and rushes, which were twisted into ropes, woven into mats and plaited into nets, baskets and pouches. Colored patterns produced by the application of earth and vegetable pigments appeared at an early stage. Lawn and gauze were woven, even before the invention of the loom—if the simple, hand-operated instrument used can be described as such. The use of the heddle, the harness that guides the thread of the loom, was introduced towards the end of the pre-ceramic period.

Wool was first spun from the coats of the llama and alpaca in the mountains. Trading brought the wool of these largest of the domesticated animals of ancient America as far as the coast. The brilliant colors and increasingly intricate patterns that adorned these wool fabrics outshine much of what is known from the Old World.

Most scholars are of the opinion that it was the cultivation of maize that first achieved a surplus in the production of food supplies, thereby providing the necessary conditions for the flowering of the arts and crafts. This prolific corn first appeared in South America towards the end of 2000 B.C., roughly at the same time as peanuts. According to latest research, Indian corn was cultivated considerably earlier in Central America, where to this day it plays a far more important role than in the developed countries of South America.

After this short introduction to the social history of the region, it should be emphasized that, thanks to the ancient trade links between the coastal region and the mountain area, a more or less homo-

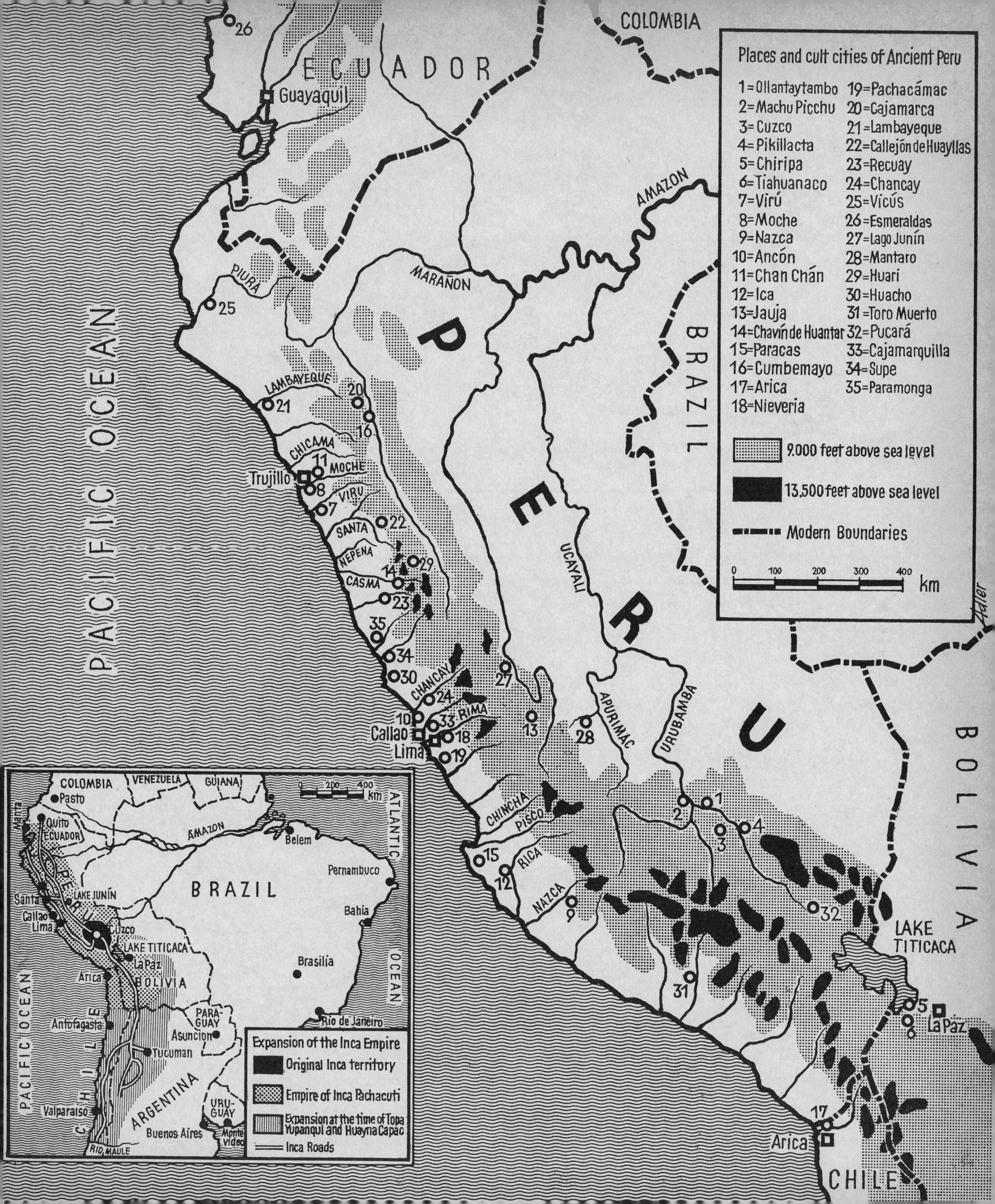
Places and cult cities of Ancient Peru
1=Ollantaytambo
2=Machu Picchu
3=Cuzco
4=Pikillacta
5=Chiripa
6=Tiahuanaco
7=Virú
8=Moche
9=Nazca
10=Ancón
11=Chan Chán
12=Ica
13=Jauja
14=Chavín de Huantar
15=Paracas
16=Cumbemayo
17=Arica
18=Nieveria
19=Pachacámac
20=Cajamarca
21=Lambayeque
22=Callejón de Huaylas
23=Recuay
24=Chancay
25=Vicús
26=Esmeraldas
27=Lago Junín
28=Mantaro
29=Huari
30=Huacho
31=Toro Muerto
32=Pucará
33=Cajamarquilla
34=Supe
35=Paramonga
9.000 feet above sea level
13.500 feet above sea level
Modern Boundaries
0 100 200 300 400 km
PACIFIC OCEAN
COLOMBIA
ECUADOR
Guayaquil
PERU
BRAZIL
BOLIVIA
CHILE
AMAZON
MARAÑON
UCAYALI
APURIMAC
URUBAMBA
PIURA
LAMBAYEQUE
CHICAMA
MOCHE
VIRU
SANTA
NEPENA
CASMA
CHANCAY
RIMA
CHINCHA
PISCO
RICA
NAZCA
Trujillo
Callao
Lima
LAKE TITICACA
La Paz
Arica
Expansion of the Inca Empire
Original Inca territory
Empire of Inca Pachacuti
Expansion at the time of Topa Yupanqui and Huayna Capac
Inca Roads
COLOMBIA
VENEZUELA
GUIANA
Pasto
Quito
ECUADOR
AMAZON
Belem
ATLANTIC OCEAN
Pernambuco
BRAZIL
Bahia
Brasilia
Santa
LAKE JUNÍN
Callao
Lima
Cuzco
LAKE TITICACA
La Paz
Arica
BOLIVIA
PACIFIC OCEAN
PARAGUAY
Asuncion
Antofagasta
Tucuman
Rio de Janeiro
ARGENTINA
CHILE
Valparaiso
URUGUAY
Buenos Aires
Montevideo
RIO MAULE
Adler

geneous way of life evolved throughout the whole of greater Peru, which we may call Peruvian, despite differences in geography and language and the existence of certain local specialized styles. And even though an entirely homogeneous culture did not appear until the time of the Inca Empire, with its public institutions, its introduction of an imperial language and its cult of the Sun God, Peruvian daily life possessed a character quite distinct from that of other South American regions. With the aid of illustrations of objects that have survived for centuries in graves, we shall attempt to reconstruct a convincing picture of the daily life of the inhabitants of greater Peru.

Peru, in common with other higher civilizations in Ancient America, lacked such features of the Old World's civilization as the wheel and cart, draft animals, the potter's wheel, bellows, glazing, glass, and stringed instruments. There were, however, domestic animals unknown to the Old World. The llama and the alpaca played an important role as suppliers of wool. The use of metals is older than in the Middle American area.

The Spanish conquest brought little change in daily life—at least not for the Indian peasants, who constituted the large majority of the population. Clearly, as a result of the elimination of the nobility and the priesthood, masterpieces of craftsmanship ceased to be made. The loss of the carefully established public institutions of the Inca empire led to impoverishment. The crops introduced by the Spanish did not, however, reduce the cultivation of native plants, such as maize, potato, sweet potato, oca and manioc, and quinoa, which grows in the higher altitudes. The llama, alpaca and guinea-pig remained the domestic animals of the mountain peoples, despite the introduction of donkeys, oxen, horses, goats, pigs and sheep. Sheep's wool was now spun and woven alongside the finer wool of the llama and alpaca, although more coarsely and less artistically than before the conquest.

Indian country folk are more conservative than any other people on earth. Individual items of clothing handed down from their forefathers still remain fashionable. The same looms are used for weaving, and pottery wares continue to be produced by the old method, without a potter's wheel. The houses of the peasants resemble the early ones in every detail. Village communities exist in scattered settlements and communal tasks are still performed in much the same manner as in ancient times. Religion was and still is closely interwoven with everyday life. Despite centuries of Christianization, pagan religious customs have remained alive. Catholic saints simply replace the ancient gods. Heathen images are referred to as "Santos"—saints.

Obviously there is no way of halting the process of industrialization. Its progress is most rapid in the coastal region. But material advance is not all. There appears to be every sign of an Indian renaissance. We do not know what form it will take, or when it will be accomplished. But it is more than a romantic dream. The imperial tongue of the Incas is not dead; it is gaining ground once again. Indian blood is strong, and Indian mothers are fertile.

The Environment
Landscape and Houses

The Peruvian landscape is one of the strangest and most magnificent in the world. Prettiness and tranquility are to be found only in the river valley oases and in the mild climate of the Andean valleys. The long waves of the Pacific Ocean, known to the Spanish Conquistadors as "Mar del Sur," the Southern Sea, bathe the shores of the vast expanse of desert that extends over 20 degrees of latitude, from north to south. Immense sand-dunes undulate like the endless sea, alternating with stretches of sand and stone, miles wide. In some places, especially in the south, desert cliffs of brilliant, multi-colored rock fall sheer into the sea. To those approaching from the sea, the landscape looks like that of some strange planet. The coastal mountains shimmer blue in the distance, their rocky folds showing varying shades of red and yellow according to the time of day. Sometimes they are covered in desert sand that reaches almost all the way up to the crests and peaks. The spurs of the cliffs projecting into the sea transform the mighty ocean rollers into foaming spray.

The towering chain of the Cordillera, overlooked here and there by perpetually snow-covered peaks, must once have been even more barren than it is today. For it is scarcely two hundred years since Australian monks brought the first eucalyptus seedlings to South America. Now the air of the mountain villages is pleasantly filled with the aroma of eucalyptus fires. The fragrant leaves and flowers of these trees provide shade, and their wood feeds the peasant's hearth. Llama dung and a form of resinous plant are still the only fuel used by the inhabitants of the high plateaux today. The quinoa forests *(polylepis incana)* that covered some of the ranges in ancient times, have long since fallen victim to charcoal burning.

Indian peasant homesteads are frequently reached by paths so steep as to make the lowland dweller dizzy. Sometimes there are steps cut into the rock; but even in the earliest times, long before the Incas spread their network of famous military roadways, passable roads must have existed to carry beasts of burden—man and the llama. Paths cutting through the perpendicular rock walls led straight across the mountains, linking north to south, some following the rivers down to the valleys.

The pepper-tree *(schinus molle* L.) is native to this region, and its clusters of red berries are used to spice *Chicha*, an intoxicating beer. It has feathery leaves that smell of pepper. Here and there the ground is carpeted with mountain flowers. Dwarf lupins and bushes of tall lupins provide scattered patches of red and yellow in the mountain grass, and in some places after the rains entire mountain slopes are covered with fragrant nasturtiums. The flowers of the prickly pear bloom amidst the cactus needles. Branches of flowering bromelia grow higher than a man.

Above the farmhouses of the mountain peasants, the steepest inclines are divided up into long, narrow fields that seem to climb straight up into the sky. In such conditions, draft animals and plows would simply hurtle down into the abyss. Here the Indian peasant still uses the hand-plow, the *taclla*.

The houses of the mountain peasants, with their straw roofs and their walls built of unhewn rocks and clay, are a part of the landscape, seeming to grow out of the barren soil. There is probably very little difference between the early dwellings and those of today. Some have survived the centuries, although their pitched roofs have long since fallen in. There is a famous two-storied house at Ollantaytambo in the Urubamba valley, which dates from the Inca period. There have always been adobe houses in the mountains, but these were not proof against the rainfall of centuries, like the palace and temple walls of hewn granite in Cuzco, the Inca capital, and in other places in the Inca provinces.

Even in the dry coastal region, time has taken its toll of the adobe buildings. The sand-swept foundation walls are all that remain, leaving us with some indication of their layout. But models of fired clay, gifts to the dead found in graves, show us various types of houses from the coastal area, dating from the earliest times. There are buildings with pitched roofs and houses with a simple lean-to roof. Complicated roof and wall constructions have inspired modern architects in the garden suburbs of Lima. Some of the walls are opened up in an ornamental way, appropriate to the climate. Roofs are pitched at right angles to each other. Stepped gables are set on the ridges of a roof, for pure decoration, as in the Maya temples. Houses of this type are sometimes completely open on one side. Occasionally the roof is supported by pillars and columns. The remnants of clay pillars are known to archaeologists. Wooden house-posts decorated with masks have been found in the southern valleys. The wooden "Stonehenge" at Cahuachi, known as La Estaquería, is famous, and at the beginning of this century there was still a veritable forest of stakes of the hard huarango tree there. It is thought that originally there must have been altogether a thousand of these six-and-a-half feet high stakes arranged in rows. There are less than a hundred there now. Many of them have been removed in the last decades, either by greedy collectors, interested only in those decorated with carved masks, or simply by peasants who took them indiscriminately as firewood, a rare commodity in a land so short of timber. Simple houses with walls of woven rushes must have existed throughout the rainless coastal region, like those that are still to be seen today. The roofs are flat and badly covered, and merely serve as shelter from the scorching sun.

The only pictures of the landscape we have are on vase paintings showing scenes of the northern coastal region, and date back almost 2,000 years. These water and desert landscapes were obviously not depicted for their own sake, but simply served as backgrounds for scenes of hunting, fishing and combat. Vase paintings of water-fowl, frogs and fishes interspersed between reeds and water-lilies have been interpreted—probably correctly—as magic fertility symbols. The bodies of frogs, realistically fashioned, sprout with various kinds of field-produce. The frog, being an aquatic creature, was a symbol of fertility. Water is the source of life, permitting plants to flourish. The desert, a lifeless land, was peopled with demonic creatures, with foxes and dragons. These creatures are portrayed more or less realistically in vase paintings, some of these as mythical beasts, products of mystic fantasy. Everyday life is permeated with religious meaning, attaching significance to the stars or the half-moon in the sky, to the blinding, blazing sun by day, or to the veils of mist drifting in from the sea over the desert and shrouding the green of the oases by the river beds, in the Peruvian winter. The cold sea-current from the south is a source of coolness throughout the year.

The whole of nature is populated with demons, half-man, half-beast. Stars dance in the night sky to the tune of pan pipes played by the dead, revived by maize beer. Drums and tambourines join in the rhythm of the dance.

It is hard for modern man to project himself into the world of religious wonders of the ancient Peruvians. This is demonstrated most clearly when we come to their concept of wild animal demons and monsters as sources of fertility. The unpopulated wastes of the landscape are full of secrets that also permeated their daily life.

Stone houses with pitched roofs, dating from the 14th century at the earliest, in the neighborhood of Cuzco, the ancient Inca capital. Stone was—and still is—the typical building material in the highlands, although adobes—i.e. sun-baked bricks—were sometimes used. The roofs were often covered decoratively, with straw or rushes, as described by the Spanish conquerors.

The most famous ruins of pitched-roof houses are in the Inca fortress of Machu Picchú. Unlike the elaborate masonry of the palaces and temples, these walls are built of rough hewn stones.

This model of a multi-storied house is at least a thousand years older than the Inca houses, which consist of much simpler constructions.
Height 7 ins. Linden Museum, Stuttgart.

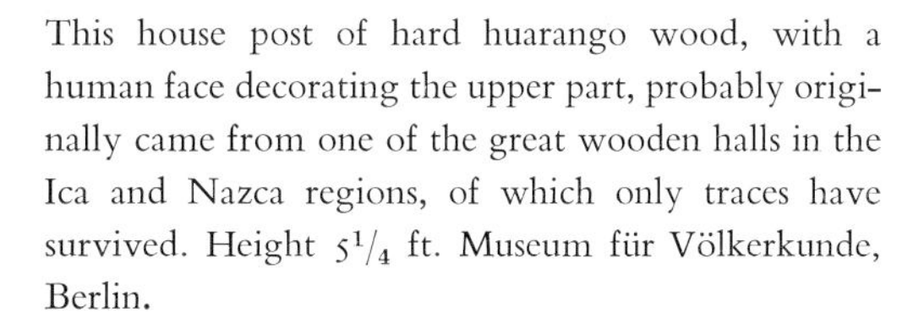

This house post of hard huarango wood, with a human face decorating the upper part, probably originally came from one of the great wooden halls in the Ica and Nazca regions, of which only traces have survived. Height $5^1/_4$ ft. Museum für Völkerkunde, Berlin.

Houses with pitched roofs also existed along the north coast of Peru, and were sometimes topped by ornamental roof decorations like those on Maya temples. Evidence of this is to be found in house models of the Moche culture (north Peru). Above left, height $8^5/_8$ ins. Museum für Völkerkunde, Berlin, and right, $11^1/_2$ ins. Private Collection, Basel.

Ruin of an Inca house with pitched roof. Ollantaytambo, Urubamba valley.

Landscape with sweet potato blooms and tubers. Polychrome painting on a fragment of cotton cloth from the temple city of Pachacamac, south of Lima. $27 \times 35\frac{5}{8}$ ins. Museum für Völkerkunde, Berlin.

Fragment of a human face. Reddish clay. Classical Tiahuanaco culture, approx. A.D. 500. Museum für Völkerkunde, Munich.

Humming-bird flying between branches of blossom. For the ancient Peruvians, the humming-bird personified springtime. It appears most frequently in the polychrome vase paintings of the Nazca culture (approx. A.D. 200–850). Museum für Völkerkunde, Munich.

Because of the dry climate in the coastal region, houses there often have no side walls. The sloping roof suggests a highland influence. Against the back wall, behind the figures of the family, is a kind of couch. Model of house in black clay. Chimú culture (approx. A.D. 1000–1450).

Below: pottery vessel with priest enthroned. The painted scene shows runners in a desert landscape, identifiable by the wavy lines of the sand-dunes and the typical desert plants, such as cacti.
Height $10^4/_5$ ins. Linden Museum, Stuttgart.

Ruins of houses several stories high are known chiefly in the mountains. This model painted in different reds, white and black was found in the upper Santa valley. Approx. A.D. 300–900. Museum für Völkerkunde, Berlin.

Right: coastal desert scene well depicted with rows of sand-dunes and cacti, with their roots. Painting on ivory-colored background. Pottery vessels of the Moche culture, approx. A.D. 800–1000. Museum für Völkerkunde, Cologne.

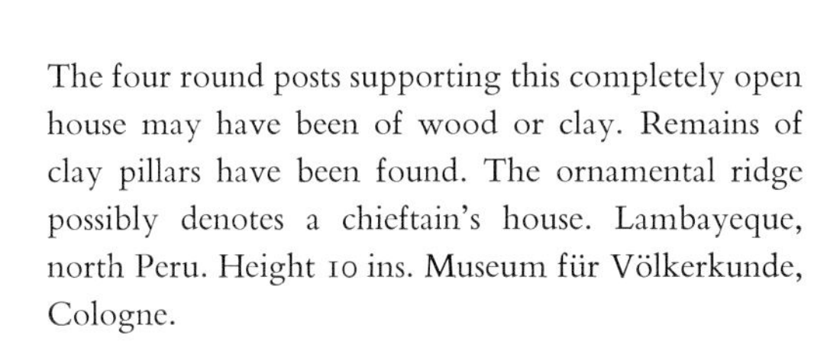

The four round posts supporting this completely open house may have been of wood or clay. Remains of clay pillars have been found. The ornamental ridge possibly denotes a chieftain's house. Lambayeque, north Peru. Height 10 ins. Museum für Völkerkunde, Cologne.

Sea scene painted on a pottery vessel of the Moche culture. Seals, various kinds of fish and a demon fisherman illustrate the northern coastal people's ancient connection with the sea. Height 11 ins. Monheim Collection, Aachen.

Agriculture

The cultivation of crops in Peru began much earlier than was generally believed until only a few years ago. However, there surely cannot have been a settled population, engaged in sowing and harvesting as early as 5,000 years ago, as some authors firmly maintain. The inhabitants of the coast, who first cultivated beans and gourds, were still fishermen and hunters and it is a matter of opinion whether the early dating given to the remains of crops found in refuse mounds can be regarded as conclusive evidence that an established form of agriculture existed at that time. It has, however, been proved that long before pottery was first made in Peru there were small, settled population groups who lived mainly on shell-fish, on fish caught with fish-hooks, and by hunting sea-mammals, but also on bulbed plants, gourds and beans. No agricultural implements have been found, apart from spatulas of hardwood and stakes, which may have been used to support plants. Underground chambers with walls made of river boulders, and the remains of round houses made of willows, twigs and reeds, thought to date back four thousand years before Christ, have been found under drifts of accumulated sand. About 2500 B.C. proper village settlements covering up to nearly twenty-four acres begin to appear along the Peruvian coast. Cotton makes its first appearance at the same time, although it is not known for certain whether it was already being cultivated at that time, or whether it grew wild. The cotton was spun into threads, which were plaited together to make fishing nets.

The remains of corn cobs of a small and poor variety probably dates back to the end of this era. The cultivation of a larger strain of corn has been shown to have emerged at approximately the same time as the cultivation of peanuts, and the beginning of a primitive form of pottery making. The harvests of Indian corn now produced a surplus in food production for the first time, and prompted the search for new agricultural land to be extended farther inland, away from the lagoons and waterways, in whose immediate vicinity the first crops had been raised.

What concerns us in this book is not so much the earliest prehistory, as Peru at its period of greatest development. One characteristic feature of this time is the harvest cycle of the Inca year, which the Spanish discovered when they landed in the early 16th century.

Each Inca month numbered thirty days, thus corresponding only roughly with the length of the months of the Gregorian calendar. The harvest year was divided into two halves. In the mountain region, the home of the Incas, the rainy season corresponds with the winter of the northern hemisphere, while the rainless winter of the southern hemisphere is equivalent to our summer.

Guamán Poma de Ayala (see figure), an Indian chronicler of the 17th century, depicted with touching naïveté the various agricultural tasks of the calendar months. The festivals of the individual months were linked with the stages of growth of corn, the principal crop, which flourishes from the Pacific Ocean to the Andean highlands, up to 11,500 feet, in the mild climate of the Titicaca basin.

The Inca year begins with our winter solstice, the time when the sun is furthest from the equator in the southern hemisphere. The main festival of the year was celebrated at this time, with processions in honor of the Sun God and Moon Goddess, when the people fasted and scattered ashes on their heads. Poma de Ayala's drawing shows man and woman at work in the fields.

In February, the month of "small ripening," when seeds begin to sprout after the first heavy falls of rain, the artist shows a watchman driving foxes and deer away from the fields with the clatter of a tambourine. Subjects of the Inca had to abstain from taking any salt and from associating with women during this festival.

March, when all the gardens and fields are in bloom, is the month of the "great ripening." Small parrots and other greedy birds are chased from the fields with slings, and llamas are sacrificed in

The Inca and his court sink the first spade into the earth, using the *taclla*.

order to obtain a good harvest from the gods. April sees the beginning of the first harvest of corn, potatoes and many other crops. The festival of the corn harvest in May is celebrated with the "dance of the young corn." The dancing and drinking is even more exuberant than at other festivals. The June festival, with the reigning Inca drinking a toast to his ancestor, the Sun God, is portrayed in one of Poma's drawings, while another shows peasants harvesting potatoes, a man with the taclla, the strangely shaped spade, and a woman with a hoe.

The main harvest festival takes place in July. The entire harvest is piled up in store-houses. In August all the irrigation ditches and fields have to be cleared. Poma's chronicle for this month shows the Inca digging the first spade in the earth, in the way the Emperor used to do in ancient China.

September is the month for sowing corn. This is accompanied by a festival in honor of the Moon Goddess, who sends rain and makes plants grow. During the dry months of October and November the land is again irrigated. A black llama is made to hunger and thirst until it cries to the deity for water. The sacred mummies of dead princes are ceremoniously paraded. "They are given food, and clothed in rich apparel, and amidst singing and dancing they are borne aloft through the streets and into the great square" (in Cuzco, the capital). Religion governs the minutest aspects of everyday life. With the solstice festival in December, the cycle of the year is completed. December is the month for sowing quinoa *(chenopodium quinoa)*, a variety of orach that grows in the mountains. Potatoes were also planted in December. According to Poma de Ayala not only were gold and silver offered to the deities at the solstice festival, but also some five hundred children. Fear of the deities dominated every hour of daily life.

Poma's peasant almanac was not exactly true of every province in the Inca empire. Owing to differences in climate and in the quality of the soil, the times for harvesting and sowing varied considerably, especially in the oases of the coastal valleys.

One surprising feature of the Inca empire is that no new crops were introduced during this period. The Andean peasants had been cultivating a rich variety of plants for more than a thousand years, before the creation of the Inca empire. Admittedly, with the unlimited manpower at their disposal and aided by the organizing skill of the high officials, the subjects of the Incas greatly increased the famous agricultural terraces along the slopes of the Andes in some places and considerably altered the appearance of the landscape. Few new major canals are thought to have been built by the Incas to distribute the vital water along the thousands of minor channels that fed the irrigation ditches in the fields of the subject coastal provinces. The chief irrigation installations in the coastal region probably date from the first centuries after Christ. The great canals in the northern valleys are famous, and were probably installed by the peoples of the Moche culture. Here aqueducts sixty miles long are evidence of the skill of these early engineers. The Inca, Garcilaso de la Vega, even refers to aqueducts allegedly five times this length. However, this may just have been a glorification of his Inca maternal ancestors. No aqueducts of this length have in fact been found anywhere.

Underground aqueducts, too, are known. Tunnels were bored through the hard rock with the simplest tools, and the walls of the canals above ground were secured with boulders from the rivers and with small pebbles. As well as the river waters, the glacial lakes, too, were exploited for irrigation purposes, and dams were constructed to catch the melted snow in irrigation channels.

After the Spanish conquest agriculture was neglected over large areas. Irrigation installations, which under Inca rule had been properly maintained by communal activity, now fell into disrepair. It has been proved that in the valley of the River Virú, the strip of land under cultivation in Indian times was almost five miles wide, whereas today it is scarcely two. When the sun is at its lowest in the

early morning and evening, in a few of the neighboring valleys that now lie barren under desert sand, it is possible to pick out ancient irrigation ditches, whose graceful meanderings immediately distinguish them from the simple, parallel type of ditch used today.

The way in which the water-courses were constructed with, as we know, only the most primitive devices commands the greatest admiration. It is hard to imagine that the gentle gradient of the canals that followed the mountain slopes could have been calculated with the naked eye. Any instruments that might have been used by the Indian engineers are unknown to us.

We do know for certain that even in the time of the Incas the inhabitants of the rainless coastal region still knew how to obtain the necessary moisture for the formation of soil, without any artificially created water-supply. This type of cultivation of the smallest strips of land must date back to the very beginning of agriculture. It is described by one of the most reliable of the 16th century chroniclers, the Spanish warrior, Cieza de León. He admires this "very strange fact that no water falls from the sky, nor does any river or stream water the valley, and yet great expanses of the valley are green with maize and fruit trees." This chronicler goes on to record that the Indians had dug a sort of pit to collect sufficient moisture for their garden-like plantations. They achieved this by removing the topsoil, consisting of barren sand, often with a high salt content, until they came down to layers of damp earth, moistened by subterranean water that filtered down from the mountains. This was genuine horticulture, and intensive garden agriculture, making use of various forms of manure. The knowledge that constant planting lixiviates soil must date from pre-Inca times. Finds of pottery and wooden figures in the deeper strata of guano islands, the nesting places of sea-fowl, whose rich droppings pile up over the years into layers yards deep, show that in the first centuries after Christ the coastal peoples were already transporting the guano to the mainland as manure. There is even a ceramic sculpture of boats landing at one of the guano islands. We know that under Inca rule a penalty was imposed on anyone setting foot on the bird islands during the hatching period of the guan birds, who were the chief source of this manure. Prudent legislation also saw to it that the guano yield was distributed among the different provinces of the empire, according to the needs of each.

One strange custom was the use of sardine heads in the sowing of corn. A head was placed alongside each seed planted, as a valuable form of manure. Human and llama excrement was also used as manure, and the fertilizing properties of lime and ashes were known. There is no doubt that in some respects the Indian peasant farmers were way ahead of their European contemporaries, quite apart from the terracing and the irrigation installations, which were so necessary for the inhabitants of the coastal region.

The most important cereal was corn, and in the higher altitudes, quinoa—incorrectly described as Indian rice—with its highly nutritious seeds. Almost equally valuable as a source of human food were beans, certain varieties of which had been cultivated long before the discovery of corn. Another important crop was the peanut. It is well-known that the potato came to the Old World from the Andes. Even today endless varieties of this all-important tuber that feeds half the world can still be found in the Andean uplands. The batata or camote, incorrectly known as sweet-potato, has in fact nothing to do with the potato. Cuttings of its shoots—and not tubers—are planted in warm regions during the rainy season. We have already mentioned that gourds are one of the oldest crops in Peru. These, like the cultivation of Peruvian cotton, preceded the knowledge of pottery and corn by more than one thousand years. It is little short of miraculous that the inhabitants of the central Andean region, with their cultivation of altogether forty different crops, with their practiced fertilization of the soil, and with their brilliantly evolved and constructed irrigation farming, should have reached a higher standard than any other region of ancient America, when their agricultural implements were so comparatively primitive, and the plow, used in the Old World since the days of remotest antiquity, was quite unknown to them. Draft animals moreover, did not exist.

The chroniclers of the Spanish conquest, and likewise later authors, were not quite accurate in describing the *taclla* used in the highlands as a hand-plow. This practical implement is not pulled along like a plow. It consists of a skillfully constructed digging stick of hardwood, with a foot-rest on the lower half. It is used only by men, whereas hoes of varying shapes are used by men and women alike. The right hand holds the curved handle of the *taclla*, which measures about five and a half feet, and the foot drives the hardwood point of the implement with its full force into the earth. Very simple sticks made from the hard wood of the carob tree were probably being used in the coastal region and elsewhere in the very earliest stages of agriculture. At a later stage prongs or spade-like blades made of copper or bronze were added. Pierced stone discs were used to give extra weight. The patches of land worked with the *taclla*, which can still be seen today in the highlands, have a far better tended appearance than those that are plowed. Although the ancient authors do not refer to any systematic rotation of crops, it is commonly practiced today, and in view of the high standard of agriculture in pre-Spanish times, we can assume that it was already practiced then.

Silver corn cobs with gilded leaves. The Spanish chroniclers tell of the marvels of the Golden Gardens of the Incas. This realistic portrayal of corn cobs by Indian goldsmiths probably dates from Inca times, too. It was found on the north coast. Natural size. Museum für Völkerkunde, Berlin.

Agricultural terraces have been preserved in the north, and especially in the south of Peru, the native region of the Incas. Many are still used today. The finest and most remarkable are the "Andenerías" at Machu Picchú, which should be replanted if they are to be saved.

Above: the old system of irrigation by winding ditches has been preserved in a few valleys, as along the lower reaches of the River Majes (Department of Arequipa).

Irrigation canals cut out of the rock at Cumbemayo, near the city of Cajamacar. Judging by rock drawings that appear in several places, it belongs to the Chavin period, during the first centuries B.C.

Below: naive drawings by Pomo de Ayala, the Indian chronicler, vividly portray agricultural labors: sowing corn, planting potatoes, irrigation and hoeing of fields.

Below: the bronze hatchet-like implement and the spade, each cast in one piece, were used for agricultural purposes. Museum für Völkerkunde, Berlin.

Simple staffs and digging sticks were used as the earliest spades. Later they were given a more definite shape and were also decorated with carved figures, as in the piece pictured here. Museum für Völkerkunde, Berlin. Copper and bronze were not used until comparatively late, and never completely took the place of wood and stone until the Spanish conquest. The spades the peasants used in the sweet potato fields were probably also wooden. The leaves, tubers and blossoms of sweet potatoes, appear in several colors on the cotton cloth. $23\frac{1}{2} \times 35$ ins. Pachacamac, Central Peru. Fragment in the Museum für Völkerkunde, Berlin.

Hunting and Fishing

Although agriculture had undoubtedly become the most important part of food production of the classical ancient Peruvian cultures, the frequent use of fish and game motifs in vase paintings and pottery is evidence of their continuing importance as a source of food at that time. Meat from domestic animals was far less important. The various breeds of llama were raised mainly for their wool and as pack animals. Only the tame guinea-pigs, that ran about in every farmhouse, were kept purely for their delicate flesh.

Judging by the vase paintings of the Moche people, hunting deer with nets must have been a sport of the nobility as early as 3rd and 4th centuries A.D., just as, a thousand years later, the Inca aristocracy enjoyed *battue* at certain times of the year.

There are two main species of deer in the Andean region. In antiquity they must have existed in greater numbers in the coastal region too. They were caught in hunting nets and put to death with clubs and arrows. Seal-hunting with clubs, on the other hand, appears to have been a sport of the common people. The above-mentioned vase paintings of the classical period (200–800 A.D.) tell us most about fishing and hunting in Peru—man's oldest way of providing food for himself, apart from gathering shell-fish and wild seeds. The oldest evidence is to be found in the middens that occur all along the Pacific coast, containing the shells of many kinds of shell-fish, the vertebrae of large fish, sea-urchin shells, and the bones of sea mammals. In the last ten years stone tips of hunting weapons have been found in the interior, as well as cave and rock-face paintings in ochre and ferruginous earth depicting deer and guanaco-hunting some ten thousand years ago. Guanacos appear to have been the principal objects of the hunt in ancient times. Countless finds of guanaco bones and deer antlers in highland settlements show that these beasts were also hunted in later times.

The masses of fish that populate the waters of the cold Humboldt stream that bathes the Peruvian coast induced nomadic groups to settle at an early stage by the calmer bays along the coast. At first

Young Inca with hunting net

Inca hunting birds with *bola*

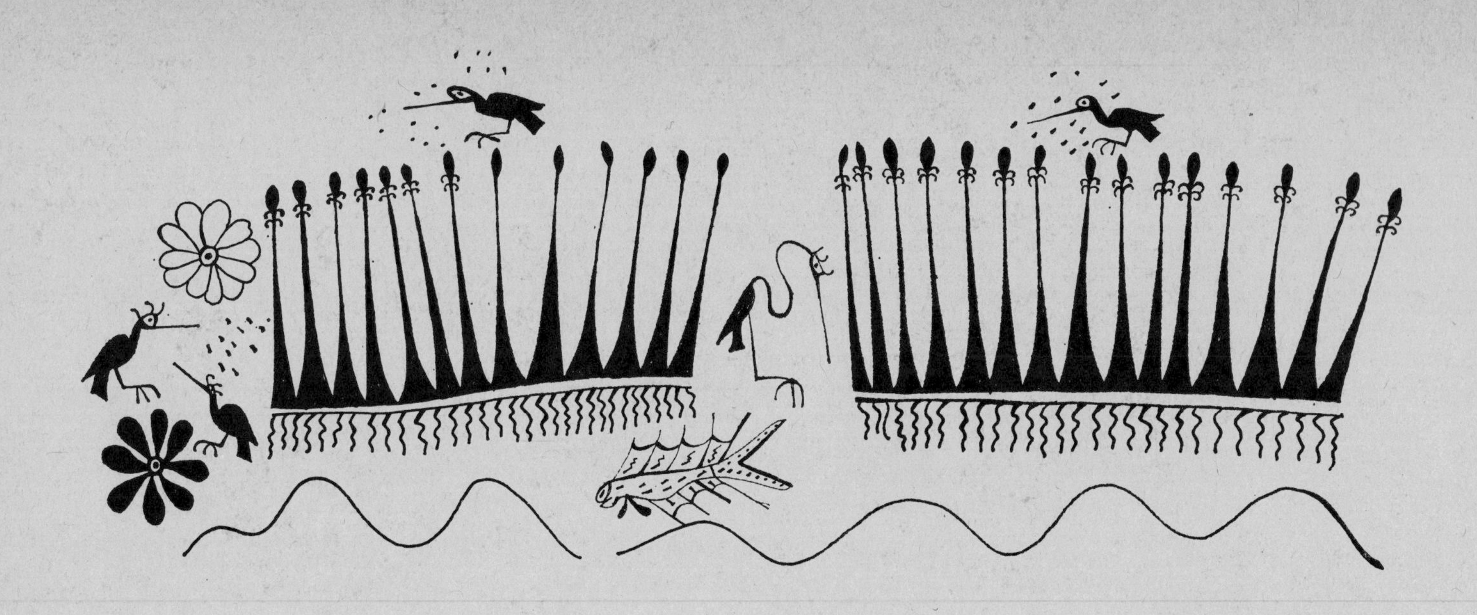

fish were speared, or caught by hand or with fish-hooks. With the discovery of cotton and its cultivation, people learned to knot the cotton threads into bags and nets, and so came to fish with nets.

Apart from clubs and nets, the other weapons used in hunting were throwing-spears and throwing-boards. Grooved bolas, consisting of two or three stones tied together with cords or thongs, were also used in hunting large game, water-fowl and the ostrich-like rhea. Slings made of braided wool, the characteristic weapon of present-day shepherds, were also used as military and hunting weapons. Blow-guns were employed for hunting smaller birds. Large and small wild doves populate the vegetation alongside the lower reaches of the rivers as well as town and village gardens, while the highland lakes teem with innumerable water-fowl, among them the most diverse varieties of ducks and wild geese. These were caught with bolas, slings and probably also in nets. Birds and rodents are still caught in snares today.

The vizcacha, a kind of long-tailed hare that clambers over the sheer rocks like a squirrel, has white flesh that is particularly delicate.

Sea-fishing with fish-hooks takes place either from the shore or from tiny reed boats *(Caballitos)*, which are taken out into the sea with the fishermen either astride them or kneeling on them. Various kinds of hand and casting nets are also operated from the shore. In southern Peru, triform floating rafts can occasionally be seen dragging trawl-nets in the more sheltered bays.

Crabs are caught in the rivers in enclosures made of reed stakes, or by hand. Fishing with nets and spears plays an important role in the highland lakes. The different kinds of hand and trawl-nets used on Lake Titicaca date back to antiquity.

In ancient times game was far more plentiful than it is today. The safety of the vicuna herds on the plateaux, which are now under official protection, was far more closely guarded in Inca times than today.

These graceful cousins of the llama, producers of the finest wool in the world, were never permitted to be killed. In Inca times the animals that were rounded up at royal hunts were shorn and then released. This is recorded by all the chroniclers of the Inca period.

Right, facing: the stag is the most commonly portrayed game beast in ancient Peruvian art. However the pottery fragment pictured here is a rarity. It is probably about 2,000 years old, for the areas of color enclosed by incised outlines are typical of the early Paracas culture. Height 8¼ ins. Museum für Völkerkunde, Berlin.

One of the oldest portrayals of guanaco (wild llama) hunting was discovered a few years ago in a cave near the copper mines of Toquepala in south Peru. These are rock paintings in red, green and white, whose age, according to modern methods, has been put at 9,580 years. (After an original drawing by Pedro Rojas Ponce.)

Two species of deer inhabit the Andes. In ancient times they were hunted with slings, spears and clubs. Hunting nets were also used. A hunting scene including clubs and nets is shown in relief on this pottery jug. Height $10\frac{1}{4}$ ins. Museum für Völkerkunde, Berlin.

Slings were the commonest hunting and military weapons of the Incas. Right: patterned sling of colored wool. Private collection, Darmstadt.

Below, left: man carrying a young deer. Pottery sculpture from the Inca period. Museum für Völkerkunde, Hanover.

Below, right: the painted interior of the pottery bowl shows animals pierced by arrows, and trapped in nets. Height $9^1/_2$ ins. Linden Museum, Stuttgart.

Hunting with blow-guns is practiced chiefly by the forest Indians, east of the Cordilleras. This multicolored painting on a cotton cloth, from the ruined city of Pachacamac (approx. A.D. 1000) shows that in antiquity this method of bird hunting was also known in the coastal region. Size approx. $20^1/_4 \times 10$ ins. Museum für Völkerkunde, Berlin.

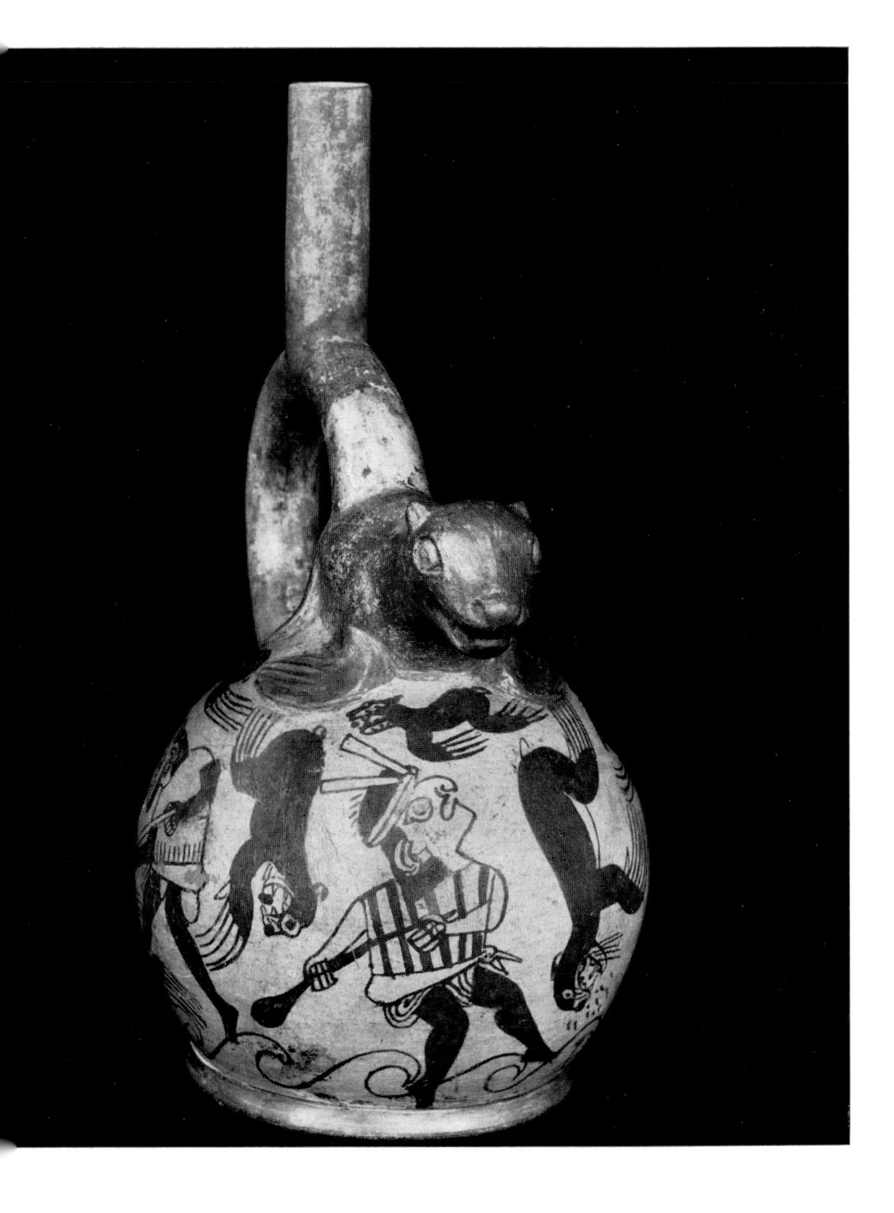

In his comparative work Gerdt Kutscher (see Appendix) has shown that, unlike deer hunting, seal hunting was not the prerogative of the nobility at the time of the Moche culture. Seals were killed with clubs. Vessels painted reddish-brown against a white background. Height $10^3/_4$ ins. Linden Museum, Stuttgart.

Opposite: angling for fish from small reed boats persists to this day along the northern coast of Peru (in the neighborhood of Trujillo). This polychromatic painting on a textile fragment from Pachacamac may well be evidence that in ancient times fish were caught by this method in the southern latitudes, too. Cotton cloth. Museum für Völkerkunde, Berlin.

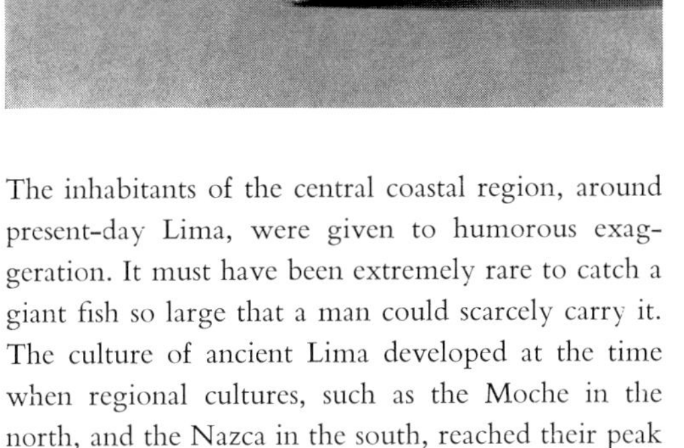

The inhabitants of the central coastal region, around present-day Lima, were given to humorous exaggeration. It must have been extremely rare to catch a giant fish so large that a man could scarcely carry it. The culture of ancient Lima developed at the time when regional cultures, such as the Moche in the north, and the Nazca in the south, reached their peak (A.D. 200–850).

Left: painted, yellowish pottery vessel. Private collection, Zürich.
Right: vessel, height approx. $6^1/_4$ ins. Museum für Völkerkunde, Basel.

The fish in the net painted on a pottery vessel (center) appear to be alive. In addition to the older method of fishing with hooks, during the middle of the 1st century A.D. fishing with nets was introduced. The making of nets developed with the cultivation of cotton. Polychrome painted vessel of the Nazca culture. Linden Museum, Stuttgart.

Like almost all ancient Peruvian ceramic sculpture, the black pottery fish served as a vessel. This is obvious from the attachment of the spout and from the shape of the handle. Chimú culture, north Peru, 11th–14th centuries A.D. Length $6^3/_4$ ins. Monheim Collection, Aachen.

The polychrome painting against a white background on this dish delights in the natural form of the fishes. Nazca style. Diameter approx. $8^3/_4$ ins. Monheim Collection, Aachen.

The double spout with a flat connecting handle is a typical feature of Nazca pottery. The delicate polychromatic painting gives a lifelike appearance to the fish swarming between the waves. The yellow, brown and bluegreen colors stand out boldly against the white background. The vessels may have been filled with water or maize beer and placed in a grave for mystical reasons. Private collection, Zürich.

Food and Drink

We do not know to what extent the doubtless excellent fare of the Inca rulers differed from that of their subjects. All that is recorded is a reference to maize beer, which was specially prepared for the emperor and court by chosen virgins, and was supposed to have been of exceptional quality. The Inca alone partook of it, and otherwise it was reserved for special sacrificial libations.

The diet of the common people was very simple. The remains of food placed in graves have been preserved. Fruit-stones, corn cobs, peanuts and the bones of animals and birds have been found in cemeteries and in the refuse heaps of private houses. Here again pre-Columbian art provides us with indirect information about the plant and animal foodstuffs of prehistoric times. All manner of field produce and animals were frequently depicted in pottery sculptures and on vase paintings. Grave finds and ancient dwelling places also tell us about cooking pots and utensils. No chronicler, however, has recorded any cooking recipes of the ancient Peruvians. They were probably just as unsophisticated as the dishes of the peasants of today.

Bernabé Cobo, the chronicler, maintains that the cooking was rather poor and coarse. Food was either poorly boiled, or, worse still, roasted over the embers, and they did not even have the roasting spit. A complaint such as this, from a Spaniard must be significant, for Spanish cooking itself, though good and wholesome, is far from delicate.

The main dish mostly consisted of a thick vegetable soup containing Indian meal, corn and tubers. Additional seasonings must certainly have included the hot capsicum pepper, of which there are several varieties, and which, judging by the finds made, was as highly prized in ancient times as it is today.

Depending on the time of year, the region, and available supplies, tubers and maize were the chief ingredients of the daily stew, which only rarely included meat. Meat—guinea-pig, llama and game—was only eaten on festive occasions, and was either boiled in the soup or roasted over embers, or sometimes baked in holes in the ground together with tubers and green vegetables. The tender meat of the guinea-pig was, and still is, considered a great delicacy. Dog's meat was quite commonly eaten in other parts of America, for example in Mexico, but it is only reported of one Andean province, inhabited by the Huanca people. The short-haired Inca dog is described as a medium-sized animal with a pointed nose and a curly tail. However, at least two breeds have been discovered in graves along the coast, one a bulldog-like strain with a rather round head. Llama meat is tasty but quite strong smelling. Llamas are mainly used as pack animals and are never roughly handled; on the contrary they are treated with gentleness and on occasion, as we describe later, they are decked out like brides.

Llamas were never milked, and dairy products such as butter and cheese were unknown before the arrival of the Spaniards. Eggs, too, were never eaten, although a large species of duck was kept as a household pet. Fish dishes were prepared in the same way as meat. To grind corn, a pebble from the river would be moved to and fro like a chopping knife over a stone with a concave surface. Stone pestles and mortars were used to pound other substances.

Hanks Horkheimer (see Appendix) has compiled detailed lists of plants both cultivated and wild, including four kinds of corn, five kinds of pulse, three kinds of gourd, and tomatoes. Native fruit included pineapple, the oily palta, two varieties of passion-fruit, and probably bananas. One of the more unusual forms of food that was eaten was seaweed, and Indians still serve this as an accompaniment to some dishes, and to this day mountain Indians make their way down to the coast to gather supplies. They may well be prompted by an instinctive knowledge that the iodine content of the seaweed prevents the incidence of goiter, by no means uncommon in the mountain areas.

Of the pulses, apart from the various kinds of beans—the oldest cultivated plants—lupin seeds were also cooked. The non-poisonous variety of yucca or manioc, and the sweet potato thrive in the warm lowland climate and in the milder mountain valleys, whereas the potato and other tubers such as oca and ollucco are to be found in the highlands. By far the most important of these was the potato, which was also made into a useful preserve. Exposure to the alternate action of night frost and sunshine, removed their entire water content within a few days. Oca tubers were quite simply dried for storage. The potato preserve was called *chuñu*. In order to make the *chuñu* particularly white, the preserve was steeped in water.

Karl Troll (see Appendix), the well-known German geographer, ascribes the military successes of the Inca rulers largely to their knowledge of this method of preserving potatoes, which not only made it possible to keep them almost indefinitely, but also reduced their weight making them much easier to transport. However, *chuñu* appears to have been known long before the Incas.

Meat was also preserved, after first being cut up into thin strips. Some ancient authors relate that sea-fish used to be brought up by relay-runners to the capital, Cuzco, for the Inca's table. This was presumably in its salted, dried form, in the same way that sea-fish is transported over great distances nowadays during Lent. Dried meat and roasted corn are the food the Indians of today, like their ancestors, take with them when travelling. As a rule only two meals a day were eaten, just after sunrise, and at sunset. On feast-days, however, there was a great deal of eating and drinking.

Pottery plates, dishes and bowls, and cooking pots of various shapes, and pans for roasting corn have all been well preserved in the earth. Drinking vessels, bowls and bottles made of gourds have naturally survived less well. Spoons of fired clay, wood and mussel-shells dating from different times, have been found in various regions. Otherwise, soup was drunk directly from the bowl, and the human hand took the place of the fork.

A kind of bread-cake, made of maize flour and baked in hot ashes, is mentioned only in connection with sacrificial rites. Ovens were unknown.

Chicha, the intoxicating liquor consumed at festivals and dances held in honor of the deities, is a beer prepared mostly from chewed corn, but also from ground-nuts, yucca and pepper-tree berries. A very slightly alcoholic form of *chicha* also figures in everyday life, for example, as a refreshing drink drunk while working in the fields.

The Spanish missionaries greatly exaggerated in their denunciation of Indian indulgence in liquor, as the latter regarded drunkenness as a religious ritual. It was the Spaniards who introduced the Indians to distilled spirits.

In ancient times the use of cocaine from coca leaves was the prerogative of the priests and nobility. Despite official prohibition, however, the greed of the Spanish planters led to the practice spreading among the masses of the common people. Chewing lime powder or a kind of cake made from the ashes of quinoa stems together with the coca, releases the alkaloid contained in its leaves. The coca leaf trade is now a state monopoly in Peru, while in Ecuador and Colombia the cultivation of coca has been prohibited since Spanish times. Some authors ascribe harmful effects to the taking of coca, which among other things alleviates hunger pains, while others minimize its effects and consider tobacco smoking far more dangerous.

As far as tobacco is concerned, none of the ancient chroniclers mention tobacco smoking among the Inca people. Garcilaso does refer to snuff-taking. However, tobacco is not known to have been cultivated during the Inca period, and this must have been a variety that grew wild in the Andes, whose leaves were also used as a medicine and in magic potions. Clay tubes blackened on the inside

Banquet in the house of a Spanish official. An Indian vassal reaches for the goblet; an Indian youth dressed in Spanish costume carries a wineskin.

have been dug up in Chiripa on Lake Titicaca in Bolivia. These date from an earlier age, and there is some doubt as to whether they were used for kindling fires or whether they served as tobacco pipes. Until the arrival of the Spaniards, fires were still lit by rubbing sticks together, and only then was this method superseded by the use of flints and steel.

Beautiful, painted pottery dish from the Nazca valleys. Germinating beans. Polychrome on a pale background. Collection of Dr. Ludwig, Aachen.

Gold beakers from Ica (central southern region) and Lambayeque (north Peru). Gold vessels were used only on festive occasions. At the time of the Inca Empire, only the nobility was permitted to use them. Museum für Völkerkunde, Munich.

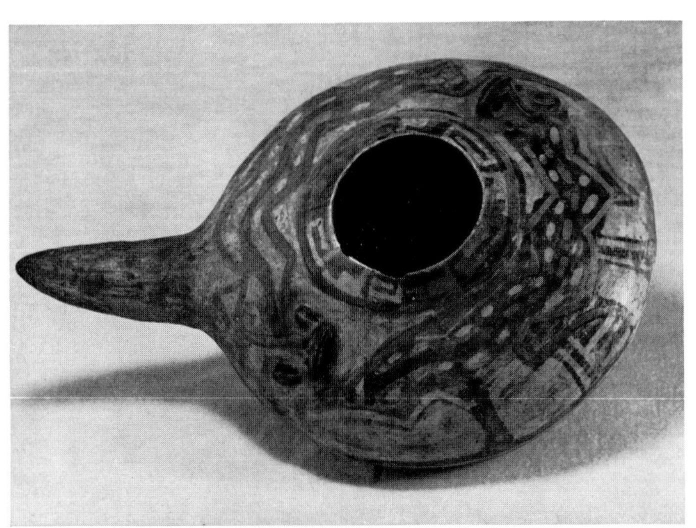

Above: the beautifully carved stone dishes and mortars come mostly from the mountainous regions, where the finest stone masons lived. 13th–15th centuries, Inca period. Above: Museum für Völkerkunde, Berlin. Left: Linden Museum, Stuttgart.

During the peak period of the regional cultures, ceramic pots with handles for roasting corn were used more or less throughout Peru, but especially in the north. This one comes from the upper Santa valley. The narrow opening was to prevent the corn cobs from bursting out of the pot. Museo Nacional, Lima.

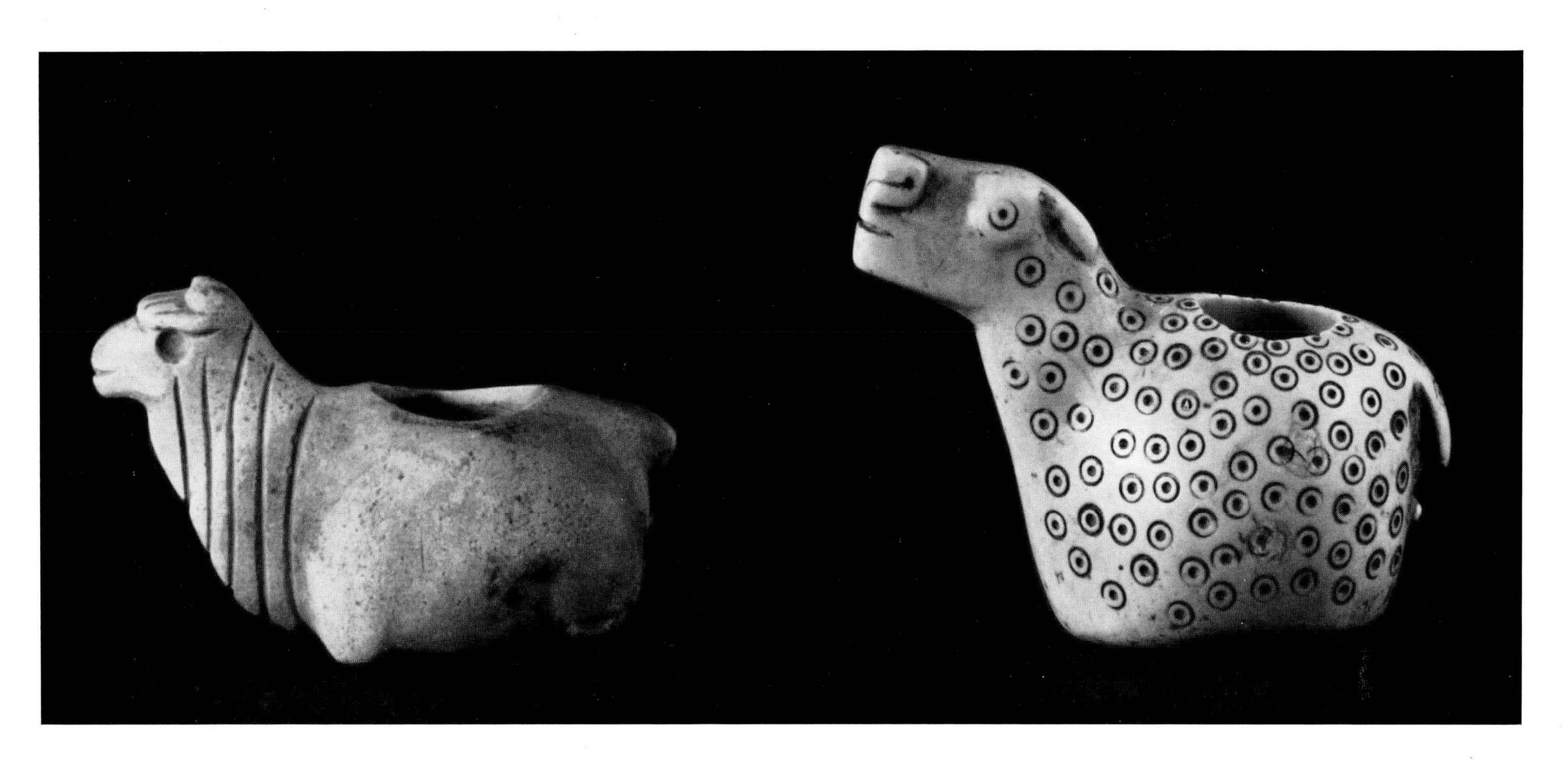

Above: small figures of llamas and alpacas, usually of transparent stone, were used as containers for sacrificial fat.

Ladles and spoons were often carved from wood, like the two above. Private Collection, Zürich. Sometimes they were made of metal, like the copper and silver ladle on the facing page. Museum für Völkerkunde, Berlin.

Left: the ceramic from the northern coastal region shows a figure chewing coca, complete with coca container and lime spatula. Moche culture. Museo Nacional de Antropologia, Lima.

Left: wooden spoon, decorated with seated monkey. Chimú culture. Museum für Völkerkunde, Berlin. Above: slaughter of a llama. Group of figures on a black pottery vessel. Ancón, near Lima.

Below: in order to release the alkaloid content of the coca leaves, the coca chewer would add powdered lime or ashes. The handles of the lime spatulas used for this purpose are often beautifully decorated, frequently with birds of various kinds. These are made of copper and silver. Museum für Völkerkunde, Berlin and private collection, Zürich.

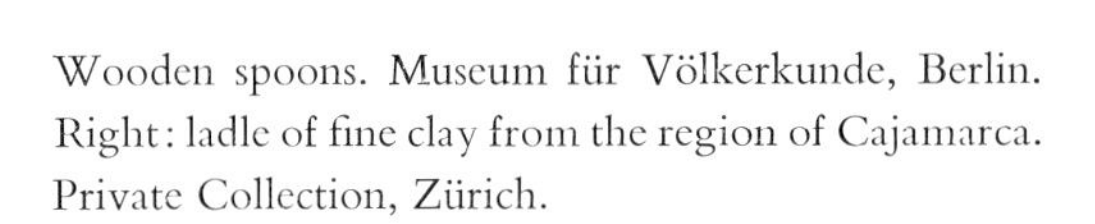

Wooden spoons. Museum für Völkerkunde, Berlin. Right: ladle of fine clay from the region of Cajamarca. Private Collection, Zürich.

Below, left: pottery vessel painted yellow and red, representing sweet potatoes. Museum für Völkerkunde, Berlin.

Below, right: pottery flask, with realistic peanuts. Peppers in relief on the lower border. Moche culture. Height 10¾ ins. Museum für Völkerkunde, Berlin.

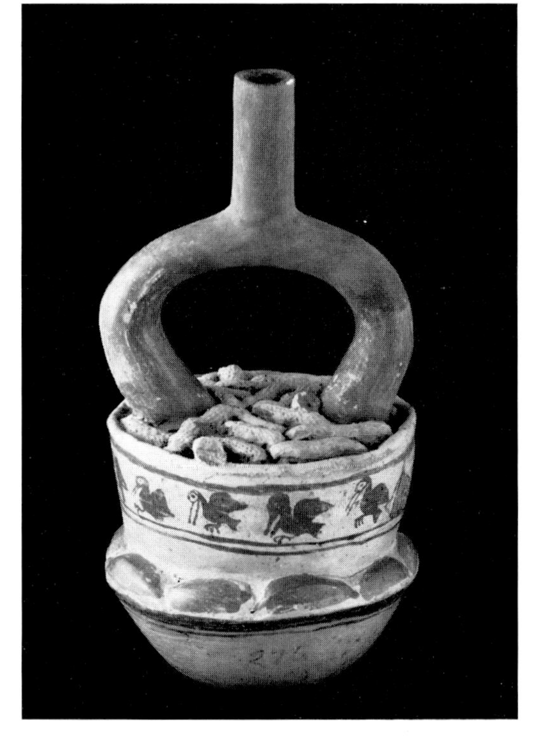

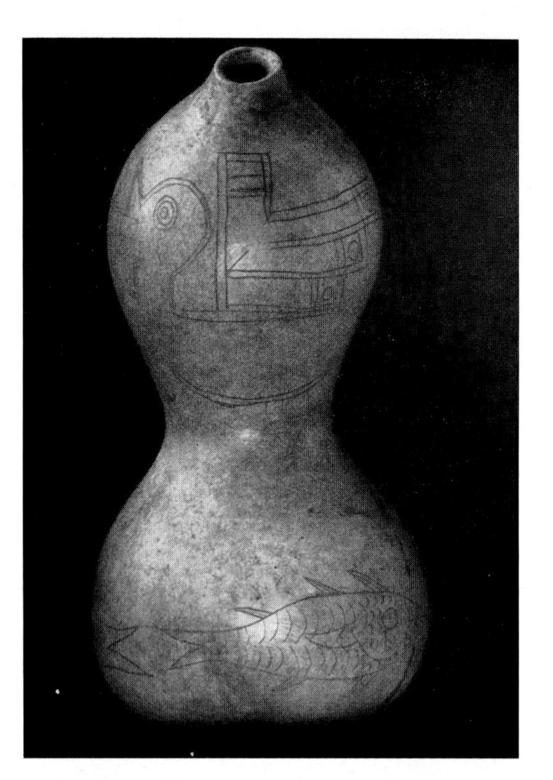

Facing Page:

Corn is a hallowed crop. Not only does it provide various forms of food, but it is also the basic ingredient of *chicha*, the intoxicating beverage that is offered to the gods, and is also consumed by man to overcome the monotony of everyday life. Drinking vessels consisted of pottery bowls, and calabashes, that were often decorated with branded designs (above, center).

Above, left: flask of reddish pottery, with corn cobs and a demon head. Late Moche culture, about 8th century A.D. Linden Museum, Stuttgart.

Above, right: a drunken man leaning against his *chicha* jug.

Below, right: man drinking *chicha* and another man chewing coca. The man on the right is putting his hand into the pouch containing coca leaves. Height 10¾ ins. and 9⅞ ins. Moche culture. British Museum, London.

Above: two women supporting a man, overcome by potent *chicha*. Two-colored, painted pottery vessel of the Moche culture. Height approx. 6 ins. Museum für Völkerkunde, Berlin.

Figure of an alpaca in transparent stone. A hollow in its back contained llama fat used in the Inca period for sacrificial offerings. This encouraged the raising of llama and alpaca herds. Length $4^3/_4$ ins. Museum für Völkerkunde, Munich.

Arts and Crafts

Until iron implements were introduced by the Spaniards, the Peruvians, despite their knowledge of copper and bronze, were still basically a Stone Age people, and as such their achievements in the artistic field are quite remarkable.

Foremost were textiles, and the magnificent cloths embroidered in brilliant colors were produced by the Paracas people in the central southern area, at the time of Christ. Only a very few museums possess examples of these. However, there are also far older kinds of knotted work with decorative designs, dating from pre-ceramic times, and the tapestries of the Tiahuanaco period (up to 1200 A.D.) are almost as splendid as the Paracas mantles. The beautifully patterned weaves of Inca times bear comparison with fine textiles the world over. Not only was every technique known to modern weaving represented in ancient Peru, but there was, to quote Junius Bird, one of the leading experts in Peruvian handicrafts, "also a variety of weaves that would be difficult or impossible to produce on mechanical looms." The same author confirms that, thanks to the extreme dryness of vast areas of Peru, the textiles that have been preserved surpass both in quantity and quality those of any other part of the world. Even brilliantly colored bird feathers were incorporated in decorative patterns to adorn festive garments. The raw materials employed were cotton, llama, alpaca and vicuna wool, and sometimes human hair. There is even some mention of bat's hair.... Silk was unknown, although the shininess of some of the vicuna weaves led the Spaniards to mistake it for silk. Cotton, was the oldest spun fiber, apart from agave and similar fibers used for rope and braided work.

The dyeing of materials first flourished with the development of spinning the wool of tame llamas, and alpacas, and wild guanaco and vicuna. Vicuna wool is extremely difficult to spin. The wool of the alpaca, which was more frequently shorn, was used for finer fabrics, while coarse cloth came from the llama. White wool is, of course, the easiest to dye. The wool from the neck and stomach of the vicuna and guanaco is white, and in order to facilitate the dyeing of textiles all-white alpacas were raised. Nearly one hundred and fifty different color tones have been distinguished. Apart from various plant and earth dyes, the scarlet pigment of the cochineal insect and the purple of mussels were used as coloring agents.

Complicated coloring methods such as *ikat* and *plangue* were employed, whereby batches of yarn were tied together before weaving *(ikat)* or parts of the fabric were tied after weaving *(plangue)* in order to obtain certain color effects and to figure the fabric. Printed fabrics have also been found in graves. Painted cloths date from very early times. Weaving was probably, largely, a domestic craft. But by the 3rd or 4th century A.D. special workshops appear to have existed in some places, as can be seen from a vase painting in the British Museum.

The finest threads were spun on hand spindles, like those still used today by Indian women, who twirl them as they sit, or walk along. The simple weaving apparatus consisted of two stakes, between which the warp was stretched, a wooden weaving sword and the heddle. The weaver maintained the desired tension of the warp with a band which was attached to both ends of the lower stake, and passed round his back. The other end of the work was attached to a post or tree. This same method of weaving can still be observed today in the valleys of the Andes. A horizontal loom, attached to the ground and stretched vertically, is also known.

It would take a textile specialist to describe the complicated individual weaving techniques. There are, to name but a few examples, woolen tapestry weaves, patterned gauze weaves, double weaves, and even a kind of velvet. The delicacy of the tapestry weaves that have survived exceeds that of the finest European tapestries. Admittedly, they were not used exclusively for wall hangings, as in Europe, but were also made into clothing.

Basket weaving does not figure as prominently in Peru as elsewhere in ancient America. Fine baskets and mats have, however, been preserved.

Ancient Peruvian pottery has survived in great quantities, although its artistic merit is not of the first order. The potter's wheel was unknown in ancient Peru, and in the rest of ancient America, so that pottery vessels had either to be modeled by hand, or to be formed in molds. The latter method was used in northern Peru from the earliest times. Where molds were not used, the potter built up the sides of the vessel bit by bit with cylindrical coils, then smoothing them with wooden trowels, polishing stones and the like, a technique that is typical for the whole of ancient America. A simpler method was to shape the vessels straight out of a lump of clay. The molds consisted of two parts. A slight ridge can still be detected on some jugs and bowls at the point where the two halves of the mold met. Handles, and the spouts so characteristic of Peruvian pottery were formed separately and joined on to the body of the vessel afterwards. A wash of thin, colored clay came to be applied before firing, if the vessel was to be painted afterwards. The finished wares indicate the kind of firing process used, and these processes naturally improved with time.

Besides painting before and after firing, other decoration was produced by incision with pointed bone implements or thin reeds and often with the thumb-nail. There were also carved and engraved designs, and combinations of painting and outlined engraving. Apart from direct painting, another technique known as negative painting was evolved at a comparatively early stage. Here the decoration was applied to the surface with wax, resin or some other non-porous substance. Then, when the vessel was dipped into a dye solution, the design was left uncolored. Once the patches of non-porous coating were removed, the design stood out in negative against the remainder of the dyed surface.

The variety of form in Peruvian ceramics appears to have been endless. As mentioned earlier, the distinctive shape of the spouts is a characteristic feature of Peruvian pottery. The shape varies according to different periods and regions. Spouts may be long or short, thick or thin, single or double. Their manufacture cannot have been altogether simple. A possible explanation for their early appearance may be that they were imported. Ceramic sculpture achieved its greatest flowering in the north of Peru, while the finest vase-paintings come from the south. Naturally, wood has survived less well and in smaller quantities than ceramics. It may, of course, have been less commonly worked, because of the comparative scarcity of suitable timber. Vessels made from gourds, which have been used throughout the ages, were even more perishable. The greatest masonry was produced in the Tiahuanaco period and during the Inca empire. Bearing in mind that no metal implements were available at that time, how the Inca masons succeeded in laying polygonal blocks without any visible seam and without using mortar remains a mystery.

Multicolored embroidered tapestry. Wool on cotton. These embroideries are genuine works of art. They are among the finest textiles, not merely in ancient Peru, but in the whole world. This one portrays a dancing deity. Late Paracas culture, dating from the time of the birth of Christ. Textile Museum, Washington.

Right: work basket containing a woman's spinning equipment: spinning whorl, skeins of wool and cotton, needles, etc. Museum für Völkerkunde, Berlin.

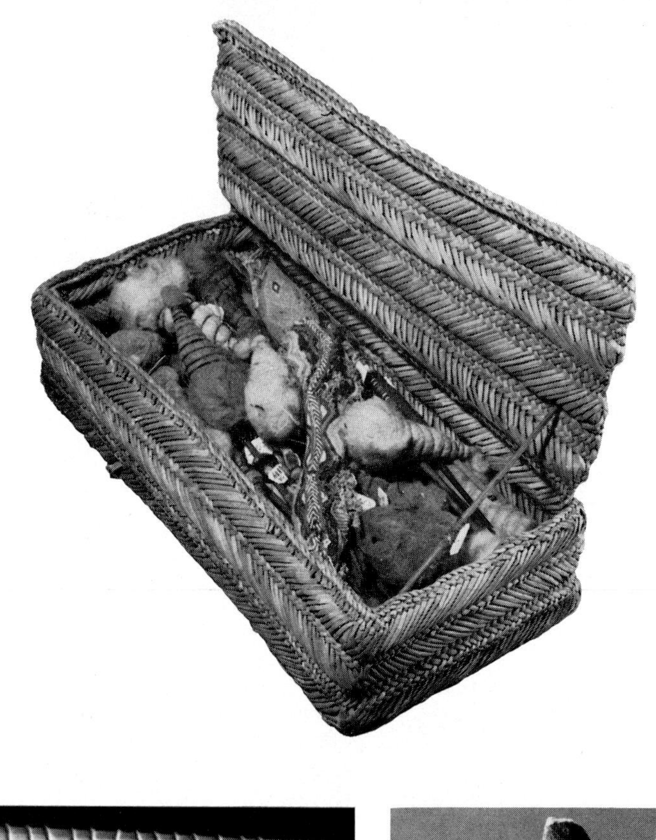

Left: hand-spindles with painted wooden whorls.

Center: unfinished work on a hand loom. Length $10^3/_4$ ins. Museum für Völkerkunde, Berlin.

Right: upper part of a wooden distaff. Private Collection, Zürich.

As this painting from a famous pottery vessel in the British Museum (London) illustrates, weaving had become an established branch of commerce at the time when the Moche culture of the northern coastal region of Peru was at its peak. Peruvian weavers mastered the most varied techniques, which are partly forgotten today.

Right: pale grey cotton cloth with human hands in broché work. Size approx. 39×40 ins. Collection of Dr. Ludwig, Aachen.

Wood was not only carved but also encrusted with pieces of mussel shells or colored stones. Resin was used as adhesive.

Above, left: small lidded box of carved wood. Private Collection, Zürich.

Above, right: man and wild animal. Carved wood with inlays of colored mussel shells. Museum für Völkerkunde, Berlin.

Various kinds of decorated ivory tools. Private Collection, Zürich.

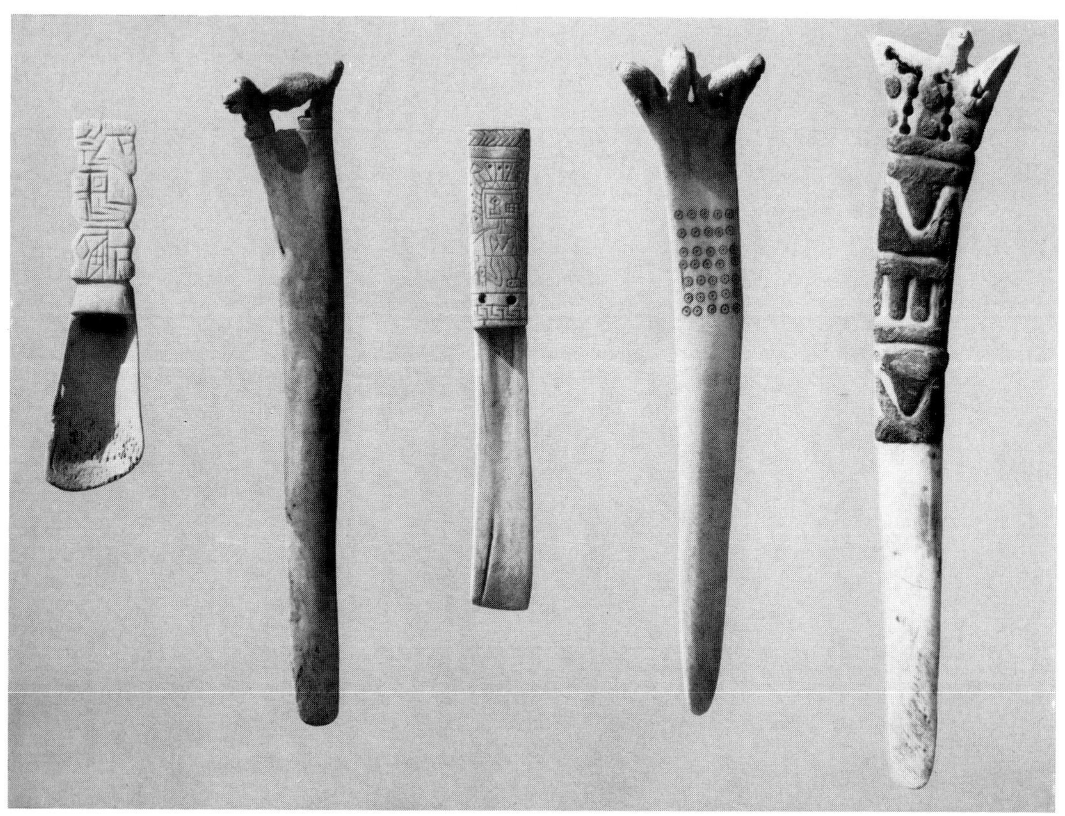

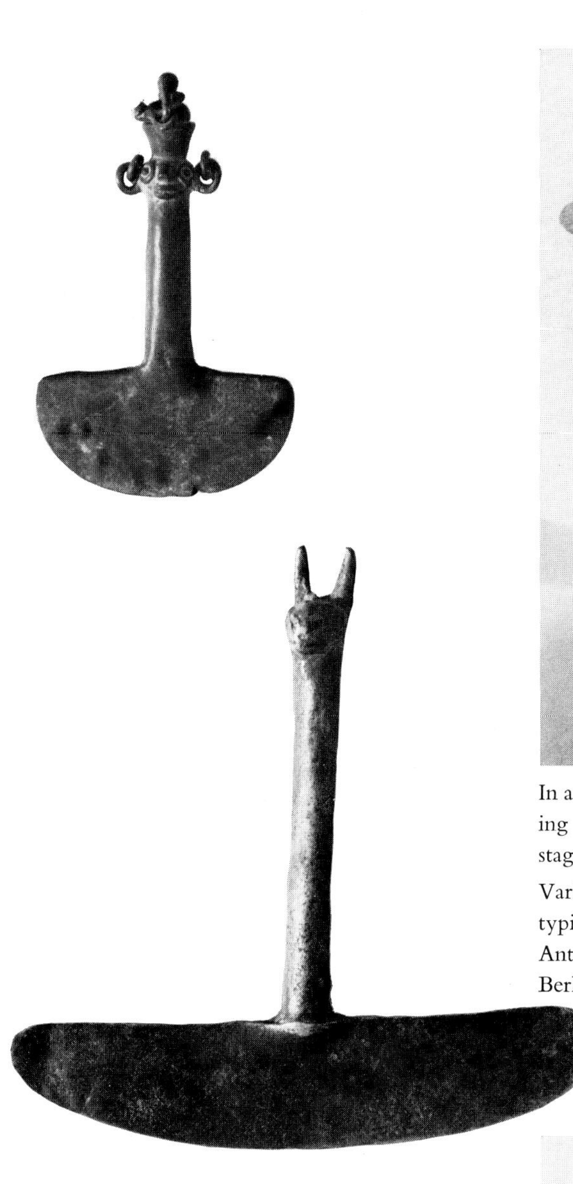

In addition to stone implements metal tools for working wood came to be used at a comparatively late stage.

Various copper tools: hatchet blades and tumí, the typical shaped knives of Peru. Museo Nacional de Antropología, Lima, and Museum für Völkerkunde, Berlin.

Silver was not used until long after gold and copper working had been established. The three silver beakers, above, come from Central Peru. Height $4^3/_4-5^1/_2$ ins. Museum für Völkerkunde, Berlin.

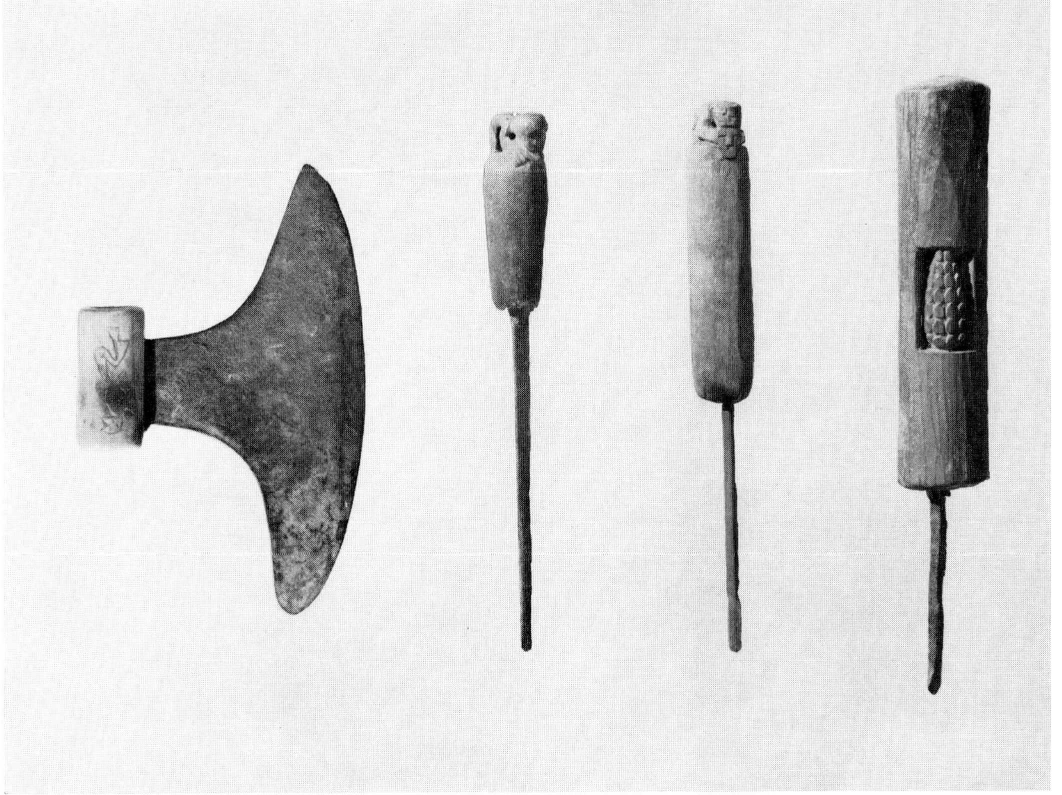

Above: double vessels appear early in the ceramics of north Peru, and the characteristic of these is that if they are lifted when containing liquid, they emit a whistling sound. Vicús, north Peru. Monheim Collection, Aachen.

Negative painting appears in the first centuries A.D. Here the actual pattern appears in the color of the vessel itself, having been blocked out with wax or resin during the dyeing process, thereby remaining uncolored.

Left: pottery vessel with partial negative painting and a group of sculptured figures. Upper Santa valley. Monheim Collection, Aachen. The diversity of shapes in ancient Peruvian ceramics is enormous. Specific forms are typical of different regions and periods.

Right: stirrup-spout flask with small monkey. Pottery with pale wash. Moche culture. Height 31$^1/_2$ ins. Monheim Collection, Aachen.

Pottery vessels of different shapes and colors. From the right: Recuay culture (upper Santa valley), Tialmanaco, and Nazca culture.

Large wooden cup painted with figures. These beakers, known as *keros,* painted with brightly colored scenes, underwent a kind of renaissance at the time of the Indian uprisings in the 18th century. They usually show figures in Inca dress or in the Spanish costume of the time. The shape of the cup is Inca. In accordance with an ancient drinking custom, they usually appear in pairs. Collection of Dr. Peter Ludwig, Aachen.

Clothing

The clothing of the well-dressed Inca citizen consisted of five main items—apart from footwear, which was not altogether essential. The loincloth worn by the adult male was a strip of woolen or cotton cloth six to eight inches wide, which passed between the legs, the two ends (sometimes fringed) hanging down from the belt in front and behind. On the coast they are rounded or rectangular, and sometimes they have tie-strings attached. In the Inca empire boys were given this garment in their fourteenth year as a sign of approaching maturity. It was a mark of distinction. Until then they wore only the sack-like sleeveless shirt or tunic, with or without a belt, which on adults reached about as far as the knees. In the coastal region it was worn shorter. The same kind of garment, reaching down to the ankles, was worn by women. It was made out of two lengths of wide material sewn together, with an opening in the center for the head. The sides were sewn together almost as far as the arms. This shirt or tunic—*unku* in the Inca language, was slipped over the head like a pullover. Each piece of clothing was always woven to fit a particular person, and cutting the material was unknown. In a few regions, short sleeves were woven on to the tunic. A kind of cloak worn in the mountains in rainy and cold weather, was likewise sewn together out of two long pieces of material, with the two upper corners knotted at the shoulder or in front. Besides a comparatively narrow belt, every Inca wore a pouch about twelve inches wide, which held food, and possibly some tools, and an amulet. Many such pouches containing coca leaves have been found in graves in the coastal region. They are often beautifully patterned, and have a narrow strap attached to them, which passed over the left shoulder, across the chest and down to the right hip.

Loincloth decorated with colored feathers.

In the cold highlands, headgear consisted of a knitted woolen cap, similar to those with ear-flaps worn today in the Sierra Madre. Elsewhere a woven band was worn around the forehead, holding back the thick hair. Often simple slings were tied around the head, with a wide central band across the forehead, and sometimes long bands of varying widths in brightly colored designs were wound round and round the head to form a turban. The four-cornered caps, with their rich patterns, often woven from a kind of velvet, are known only in the Tiahuanaco period. Judging by the ceramic figures from the northern coastland the most diverse forms of headgear were worn there, not only turbans and simple head-bands, but also feathers, and animal skins. The turbans and head-bands were occasionally worn with fan-shaped feathered headdresses or ornamental metal combs. The women often wore a special kind of folded cloth on the head, which also shielded the neck.

Most of the articles of clothing mentioned, the loincloth, tunic and belt had been standard wear since the time of Christ, with only minor variations regarding, for example, the length of the tunic.

The representations of human figures dating from the centuries before Christ show only the loincloth and the belt, and a helmet-like headdress. The upper part of the body was naked.

Graves contain little by way of footwear—occasionally sandals made of rawhide, with woolen tie-laces have been found, and in some areas woolen moccasins.

The Inca women wore wrap-around skirts held up by belts, and coats made of rectangular pieces of material, that were longer than the men's, reaching down to the ankles. Their cloaks were fastened across the breast by long metal brooches, or quite often by simple bone pins or even thorns. Shawls, *(llicllas)* were also used to carry lighter burdens. Babies were probably carried on the back in these shawls, just as they are today by the Indian women. The women's clothing also included small bags. Women usually wore their hair long, often parted in the middle and plaited into one or more braids, while the male subjects of the Inca cut their hair with obsidian knives. Men are also depicted with long hair. Occasionally several hair-styles appear to have been fashionable in one and the same region, as can be seen from the heads of mummies from the central coastland.

Men's and women's combs consisted of two rows of teeth made of thorns and held in position by a small strip of cloth in the middle. Sometimes it appears to have been the custom to dye the hair. On certain occasions, such as in war and mourning, the face and body were painted with earth and vegetable pigments. The Indians removed their scanty beard growth with small tweezers, originally made of mussel shells and later of metal. A few of the beard tweezers that have been found, have a small hole at the top, so that they could be threaded on a string and worn round the neck.

Woman weaving, dressed in typical woman's costume

Inca official in long tunic and mantle

This type of four-cornered hat, made in a variety of fabrics, sometimes even in a kind of velvet or plush, belongs to the Tiahuanaco culture which spread through the whole of Peru during the 9th–12th centuries A.D. The fine wool gives the rich colors a special sheen. Museum für Völkerkunde, Berlin.

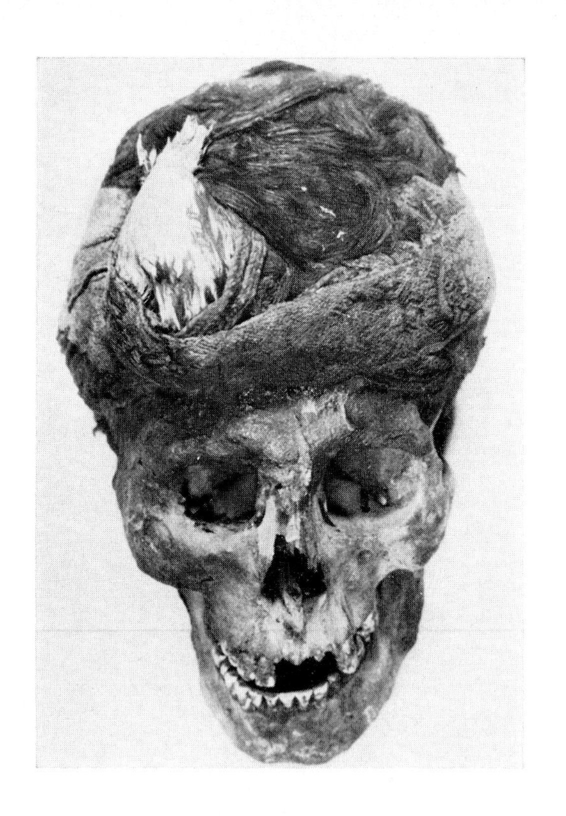

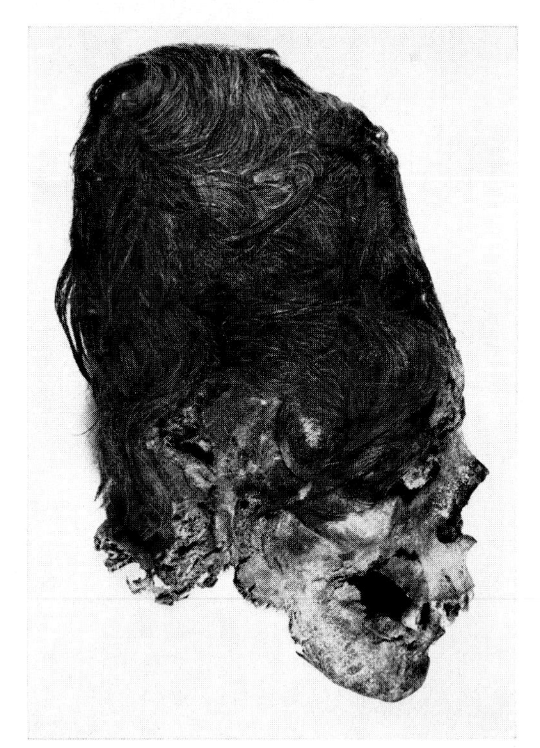

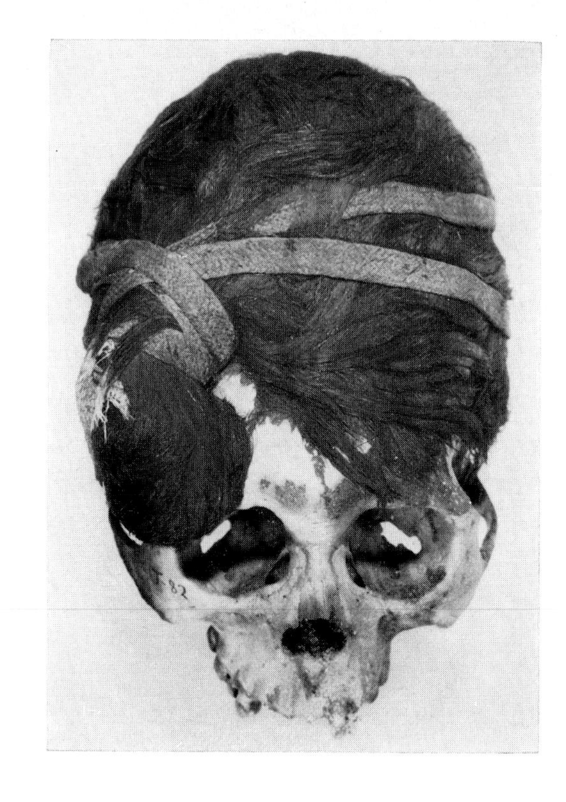

In the course of time, men's and women's hairstyles evolved from one or more braids to a short haircut. Our knowledge of the hairstyles of certain periods comes from mummified heads, which were best preserved in the region of Nazca and Ica. They may be styles peculiar to certain social ranks or noble families. Head-bands of various kinds or turbans of colored cords and woven braids were popular. Museo de Antropología, Ica.

In the earliest times, tweezers for the removal of the Indians' sparse beard and body hairs were simply made out of two mussel shells. Later, small and large metal tweezers were used, made of gold, silver and copper. Center and below: silver tweezers for removing hair. Museum für Völkerkunde, Berlin.

Four-cornered caps also appeared along the coast during the Tiahuanaco period. The mountain people wore a kind of cap with earflaps, similar to that which is still worn today by the Indians on the high plateaux. Turbans of wool or cotton bands were commonly worn in the coastal region at the time of the birth of Christ. Combs were mostly made from cactus spines bound together. Two-sided combs were the more usual.

Right: Museum für Völkerkunde, Munich. Below, left: Museum für Völkerkunde, Berlin. Below, right: Museo Nacional, Lima.

Below: the pattern on this fragment of a tunic from the coastal area (Chimú culture) simulates hanging metal plates. The colors are red and yellow. Private Collection, Zürich.

Attached to the top of this loin cloth are tie-strings which were bound round the body. The fringed end hung down loose at the back. Museum für Völkerkunde, Munich.

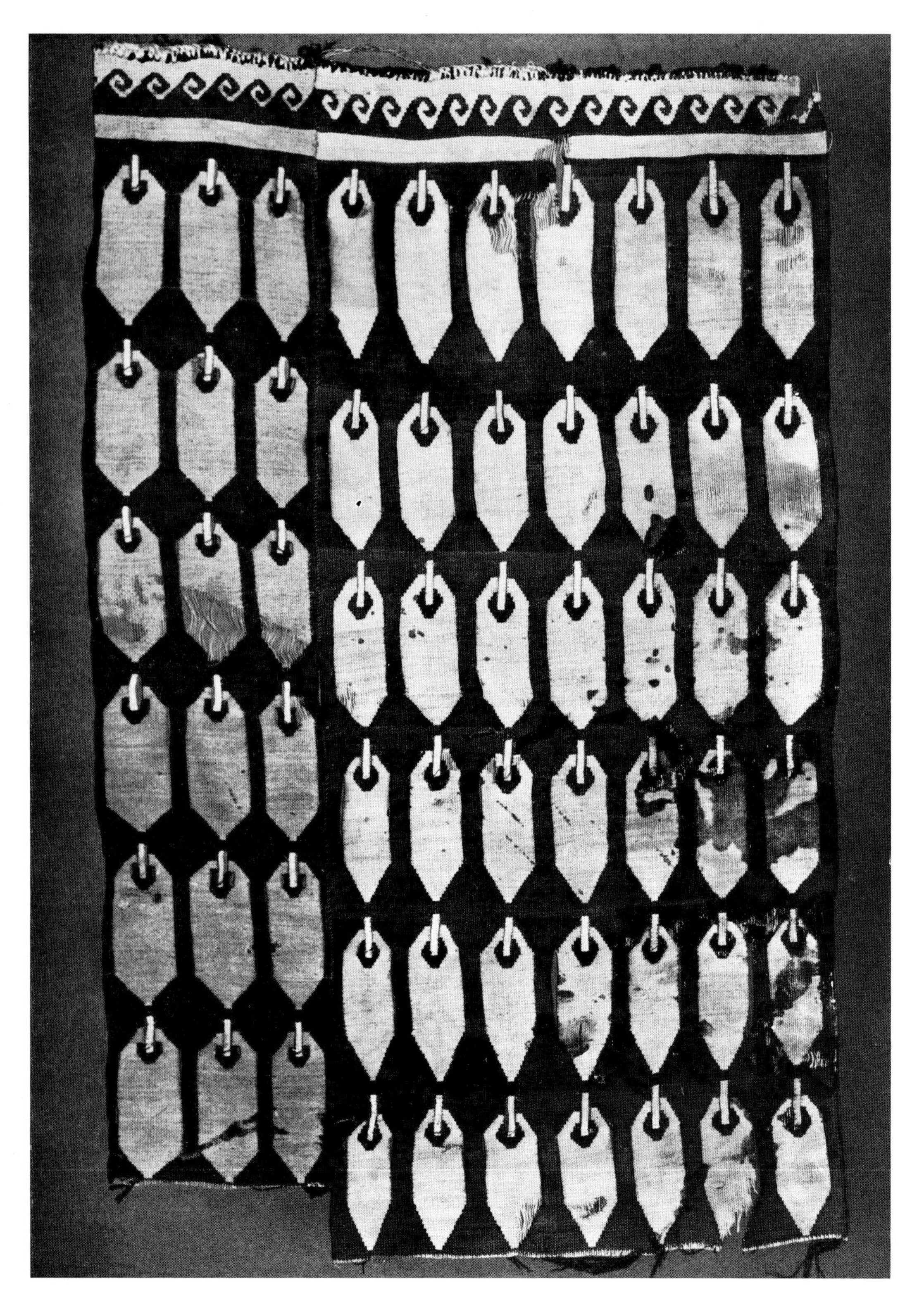

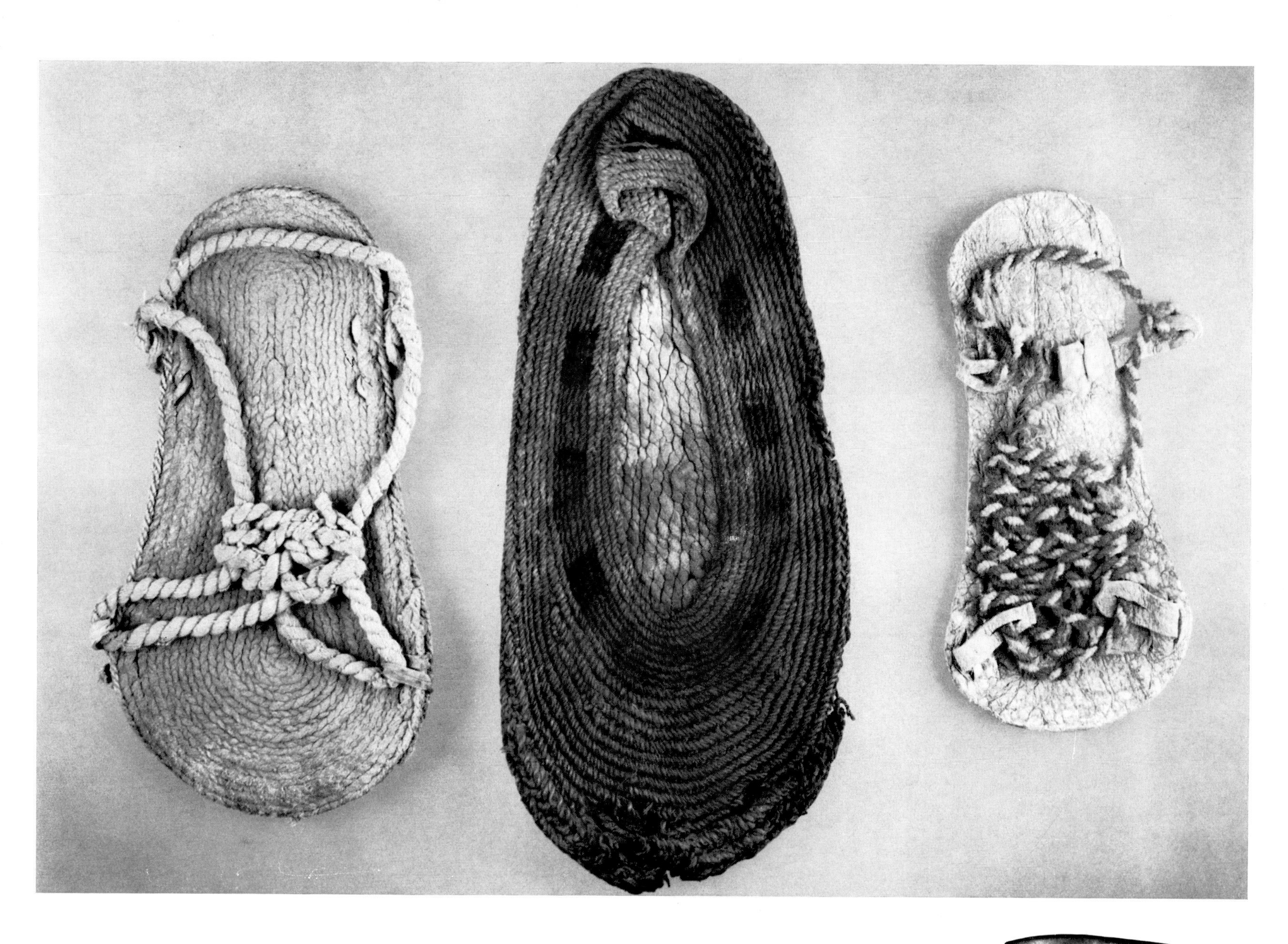

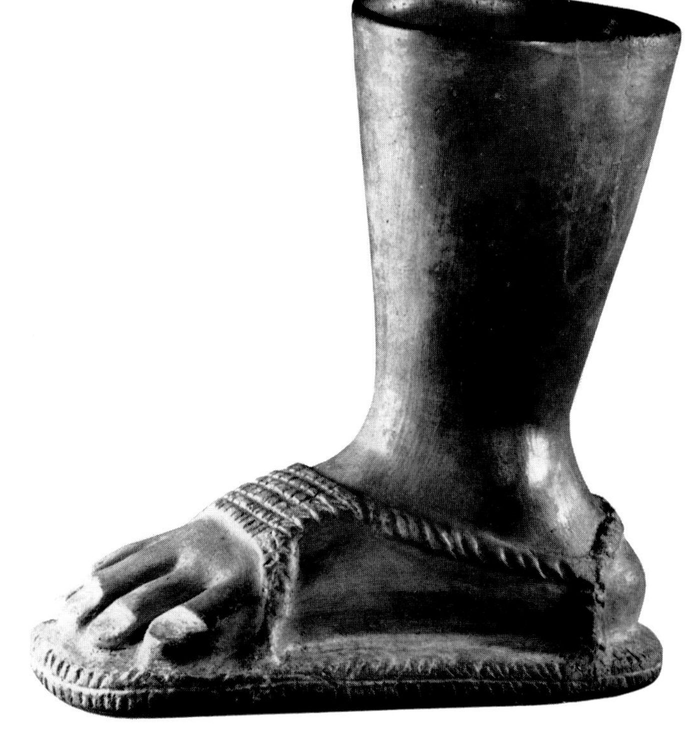

Above: there were two main types of footwear—sandals and moccasins. The moccasin (center) comes from Nazca, the sandal from Pachacamac. Worked in wool, cotton and leather. Museum für Völkerkunde, Berlin.

Right: foot with sandal. Reddish clay. Inca period. Museum für Völkerkunde, Berlin.

Tunic from the Inca period. The chessboard pattern appears to have been a kind of uniform of the Inca warrior. Neck border of gold beads of varying shapes and sizes.

Gold and Jewelry

Gold, in terms of property, or jewelry was, as mentioned earlier, of little significance for the general populace before the arrival of the Spaniards. It is said that in Inca times only the princes were allowed to adorn themselves with gold. Garcilaso de la Vega, the Inca chronicler, however, maintains that this prohibition was not introduced until the reign of the great Inca reformer, Pachacutic Inca Yupanqui (1438–1471). Most of the gold seized by the Spaniards was in fact taken from palaces and temples. Gold was sacred to the Sun God, and silver to the Moon Goddess. Temple walls and the walls of palaces were hung with sheets of gold and silver. There is no word in the Inca imperial language to lead us to suppose there was any mystical regard for gold, such as in Mexico, where gold was known as "excrement of the gods" (Teocuitlatl). Yet, the goldsmith's art is much older in Peru than in Central America, and the weight of evidence suggests that metal working as a whole originated in Peru or in Colombia. Again, of all the metals worked, gold is the oldest. In the north of Peru, the earliest pieces of jewelry, made of hammered gold, date back centuries before Christ. The gold of Peru became proverbial after the conquest,—"Vale un Peru" was a common expression in Spanish. Of the gold and silver figures and vessels listed in the Indian Archive in Seville as tributes delivered to the Spanish throne by the brothers Pizarro and their comrades in arms (the levy of one-fifth of the booty payable by law), not a single piece remains today. The Spanish chroniclers relate that, after the execution of the Inca Atahualpa (1533), fires were kept burning day and night for a whole month under earthenware crucibles, on the hills near the town of Cajamarca, in order to melt down the gold booty into bars. Indian goldsmiths were compelled to perform this destructive task themselves. The wind that swept over the hills acted like bellows, which at that time were unknown. Whenever the wind dropped, tubes were used to fan the fires.

To form some idea of the fabulous treasure destroyed by the Spaniards, one has only to read the accounts of the golden gardens. A few sentences from Garcilaso's commentaries are appropriate at this point: "In these gardens there were also animals of every variety, of gold and silver. There were birds sitting on the trees. . . . There was maize with stalks of silver and cobs of gold, complete with leaves and grains and even their flower panicles. . . ."

But a thousand times more gold than ever the Spaniards melted down, still emerges today from ancient graves. Treasure seekers are forever burrowing in the earth in their search for the gold of the dead. Gold was washed out of the sand of the rivers. The few gold mines that existed all lay close to the surface. Gold was not only used for jewelry, but also for implements—golden beard tweezers, fish-hooks of pure gold, and gold stars shaped to fit club heads—not to mention light and heavy gold tableware. Museums display necklaces of hollow gold beads, often decorated with carved figures, complete pendants, with huge centerpieces, small idols, gold bracelets, mummy masks of gold, even gold gloves for the dead. Gold fingernails have been found attached to bodies.

There are half-moon shaped nose ornaments, earrings, ear pendants, and huge mushroom-shaped ornaments that must have pulled heavily on the pierced ear-lobe. The front disc is often embossed in relief, or occasionally inlaid with turquoise or mussel shells. Ear-plugs with colored feather mosaics or inlays of different colored mussel shells have been dug out of graves. They come in part from the northern coast, but mostly from the central coast.

Hammering and engraving were the oldest ways of working gold, and persisted until the time of the Incas. The casting of gold and the making of alloys of gold with silver or copper appeared early on. Platinum and an alloy of gold and platinum is known only in Ecuador. The technique of working platinum was known there much earlier than in the Old World. Jewelry hammered and cut from sheets of gold comes chiefly from the south of Peru.

Gold beaker, decorated with embossed birds and human heads

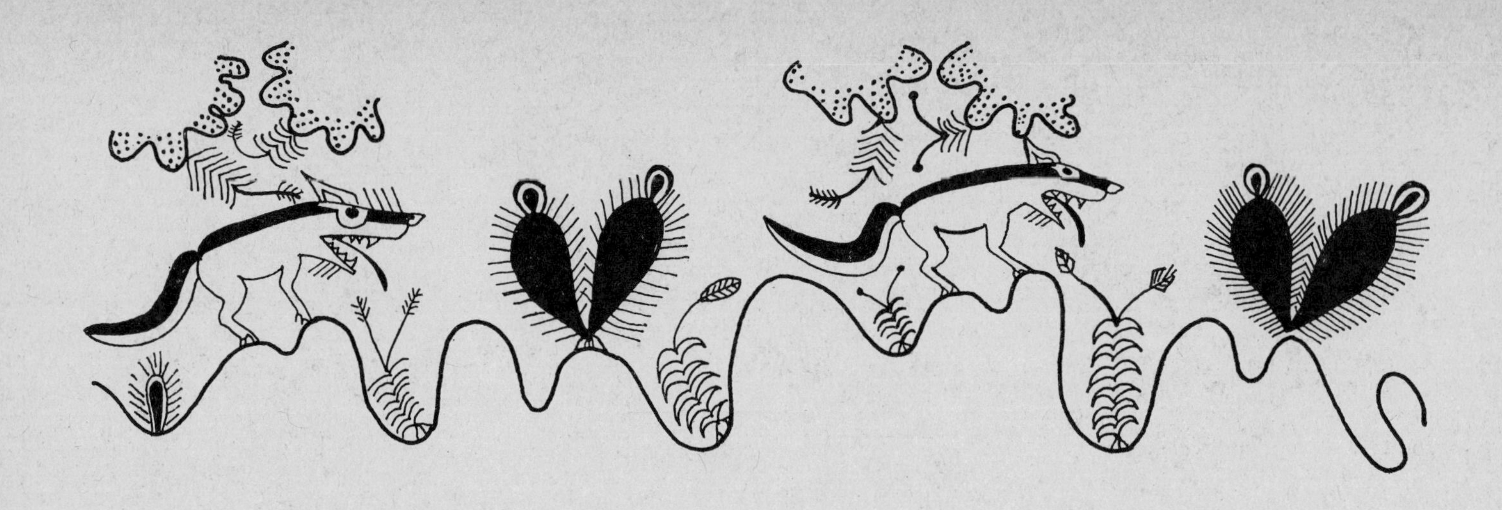

Finger rings of bone have been found in graves of earlier cultures in the northern coastal region. The dead wore four such bone rings on the fingers of one hand. Rings appear to have been worn less in later times.

The earliest jewelry was made from suitable seeds and the stones of fruit, from wood and mussel-shells, and later also from clay. These materials were made into necklaces, bracelets, and into adornments for clothes. Semi-precious stones, such as turquoise and lapis lazuli, and even hard rock-crystal were polished and pierced for threading. Emeralds came from Colombia.

Certain ornaments are known to have had special significance as amulets. The ear-plugs mentioned earlier, made of gold, wood or clay, could only be worn by those of high rank in the Inca empire. The Spanish name for the nobility—"Orejones" (Great Ears)—derives from this. The same custom probably existed much earlier in the north of Peru. It is recorded that, on reaching puberty, the youths of the Inca nobility had their ears pierced to take these ear-plugs, which conferred on them the status of warriors.

The nose ornaments appear to have been restricted to certain regions, and the lip adornments to one small area in the north.

The largest finds of gold were made, probably already in Spanish times, in the residence of the minor kings of the Chimú and in the sanctuaries and graves of Chanchan. In the nineteen-twenties rich finds of gold treasure were made even farther north. The grave of a single man apparently contained funerary gifts of more than one hundred engraved gold beakers. His grave at Batan Grande near Lambayeque was plundered only a few years ago, after rich finds of gold, including masks in an unusual style and knives with figure designs, had earlier been made in the same area. These precious objects are owned by the National Museum of Lima and by a few private collectors.

In the last few years, the hunt for gold has led plunderers to an entirely new area in the extreme north of Peru. Vessels, figurines, breastplates and innumerable nose ornaments have been found there. Many of the gold articles have a high copper content. There is also a surprising amount of gilding. Various gilding techniques were known in Peru, including leaf-gilding, hot-gilding, as well as the "mis-en-couleur" process, whereby objects made of gold alloys with a high copper content were treated with vegetable juices containing oxalic acid, which ate away the copper, leaving a thin coating of pure gold on the surface.

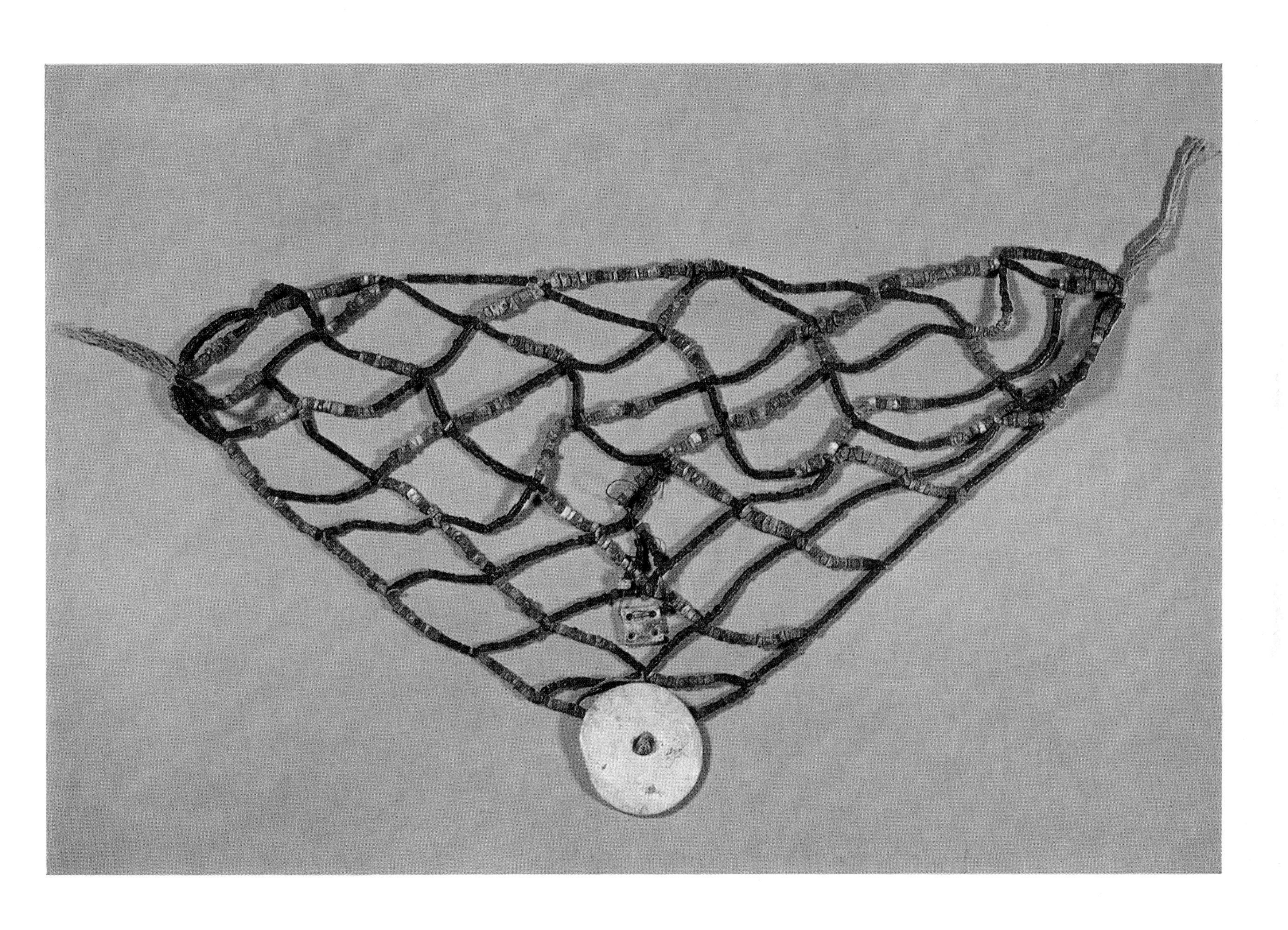

Bead necklaces are rarely preserved in their original form, since the strings are often torn, and the finders—mostly treasure seekers, string the loose beads together more or less arbitrarily. Obviously, this does not happen with careful excavation. Museum für Völkerkunde, Berlin.

There are mummy masks of wood, pottery and metal. Masks of thin gold plate, sometimes painted red, have survived chiefly in the north of the Peruvian coastal strip. The almond-shaped eyes are characteristic of the Lambayeque region (north Peru). Height approx. $4^3/_8$ ins. Private Collection, U.S.A.

Nose ornaments, too, were worn mainly in the northern coastal region of Peru, as well as in the neighboring countries of Ecuador and Colombia. The ornaments are of thick, gold plate, with a spiral-shaped design cut out of them. Weight 64 and 66.2 grammes. The specimens pictured above consist of one gold half and one silver half riveted together. They were all found at Vicús, near the town of Piura (north Peru), a site that was only discovered a few years ago. Collection of Dr. Ludwig, Aachen.

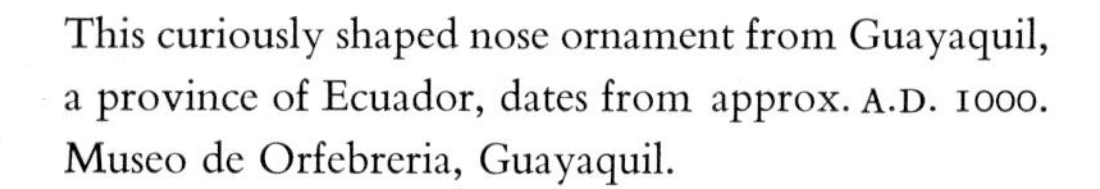
This curiously shaped nose ornament from Guayaquil, a province of Ecuador, dates from approx. A.D. 1000. Museo de Orfebreria, Guayaquil.

The ear-plugs, right, which were worn in the pierced lobe of the ear, with the decorated side to the front, each consist of four parts. Thin gold plate. Weight 13 and 14 grammes. Height $1^{5}/_{8}$ ins.

The beads of this necklace are hollow and each consists of two halves. The arrangement of the large and small beads appears to be quite original. North Peruvian coastal region. Weight 54.1 grammes. Collection of Dr. Ludwig, Aachen.

The ornamental pendant, made of gold and platinum alloy, comes from the gold province of Esmeralda (Ecuador). Museo de Orfebreria, Guayaquil. The working of platinum was known here centuries earlier than in Europe.

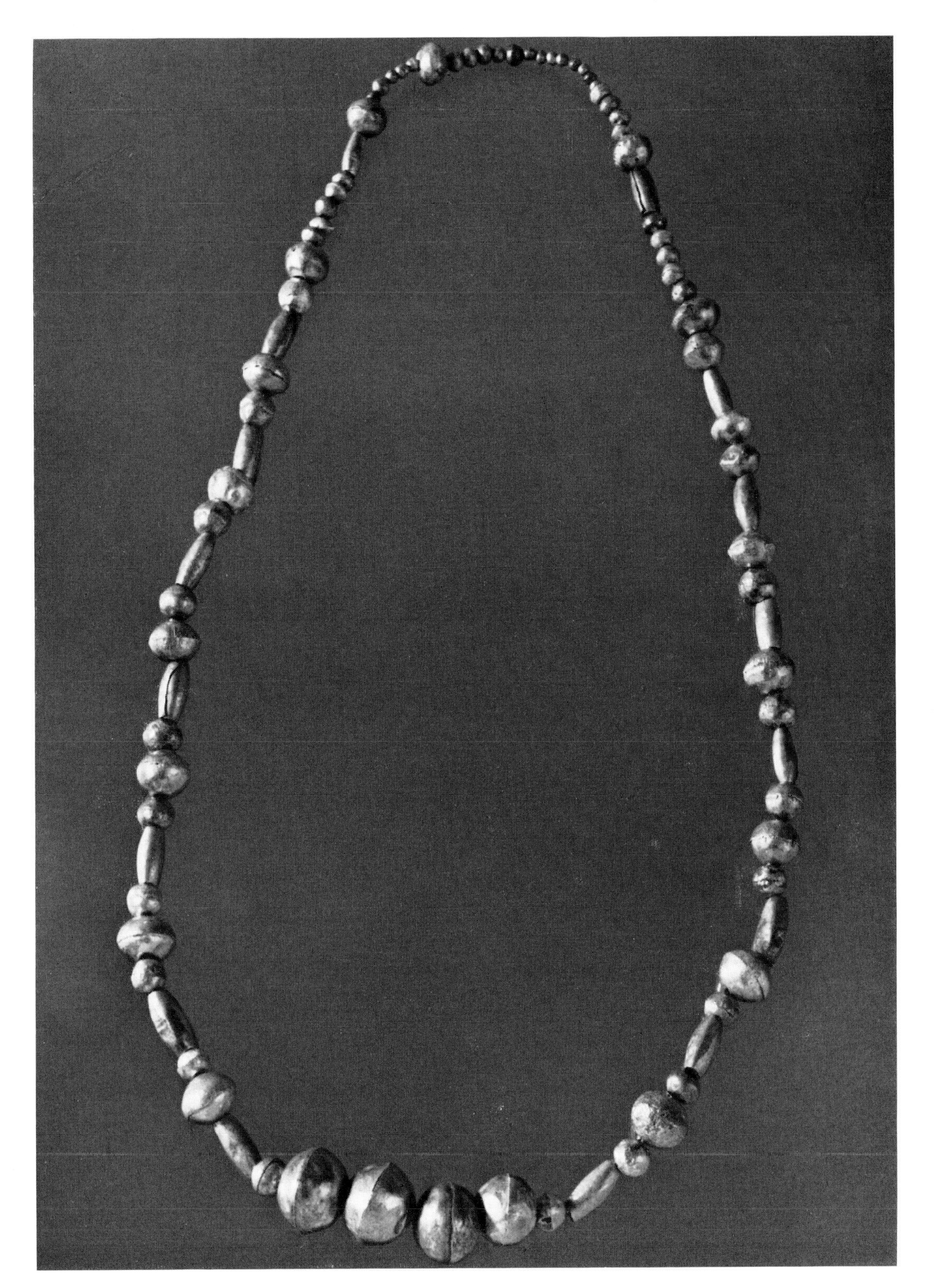

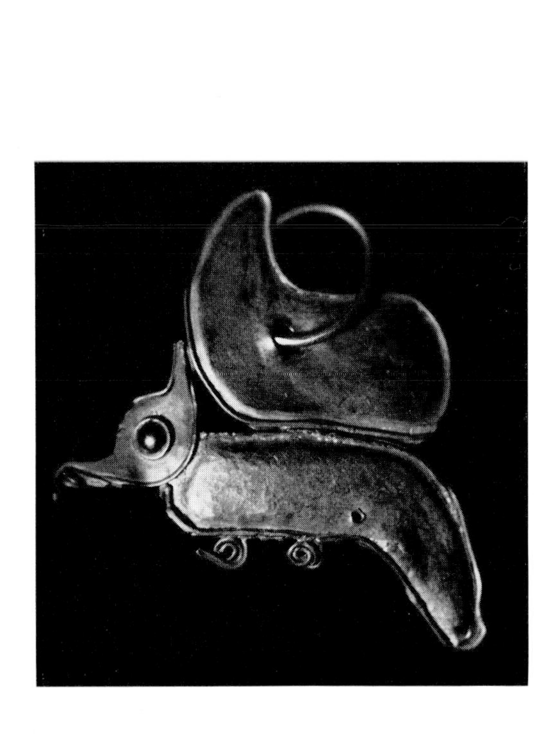

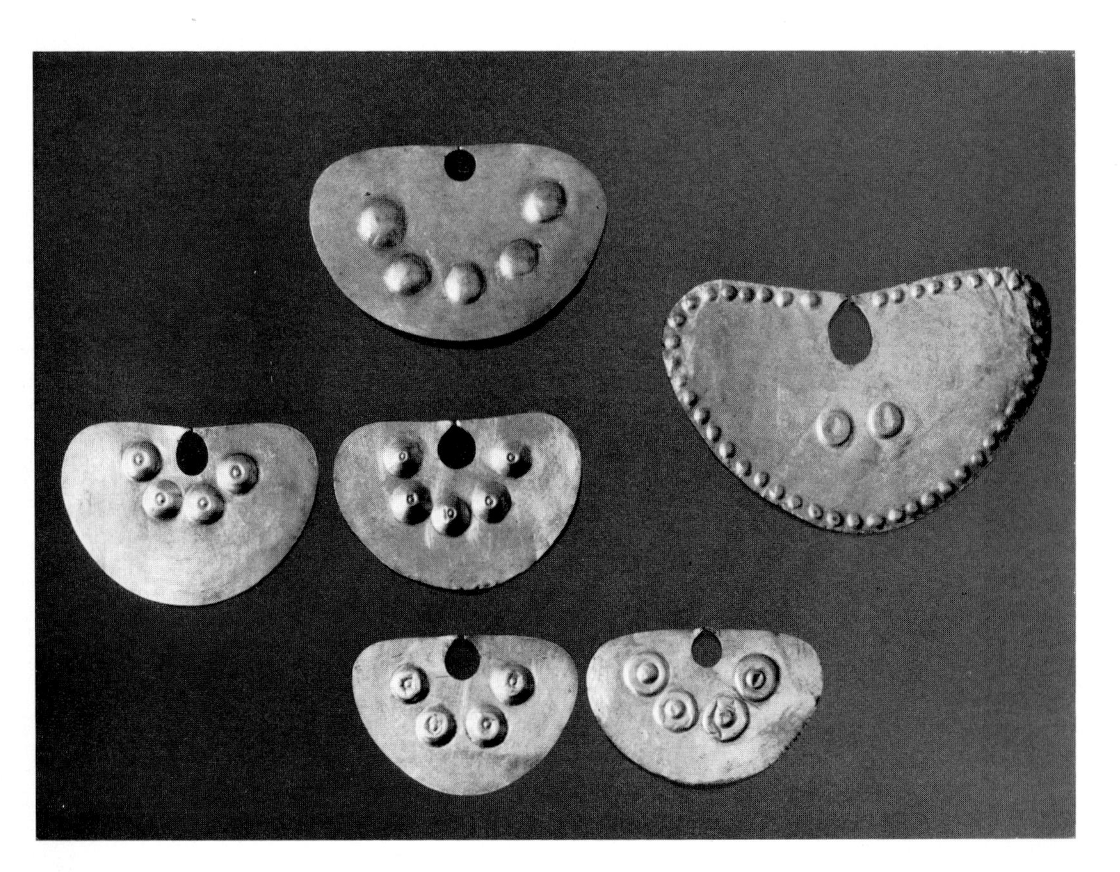

The golden nose ornament comes from the province of Guayaquil in Ecuador. Weight 118 grammes. Museo de Orfebreria, Guayaquil.

The simpler nose ornaments of gold plate with embossed rosettes are typical of the site of Vicús, where they were found (north Peru). Weight 3.4 and 4.4 grammes.

Above: dress adornment of gold with a silver content, with animal heads and bells. Lambayeque. Collection of Dr. Ludwig, Aachen.

The scene of combat engraved on the pair of ear-plugs, right, is in typical Moche style. Private Collection, Zürich.

This ornamental piece of jewelry was sewn onto a costume. The design is cut away, and shows a hunting scene, with flute players and stags. Width $7^{1}/_{4}$ ins. Weight 21.5 grammes. Vicús style. Collection of Dr. Ludwig, Aachen.

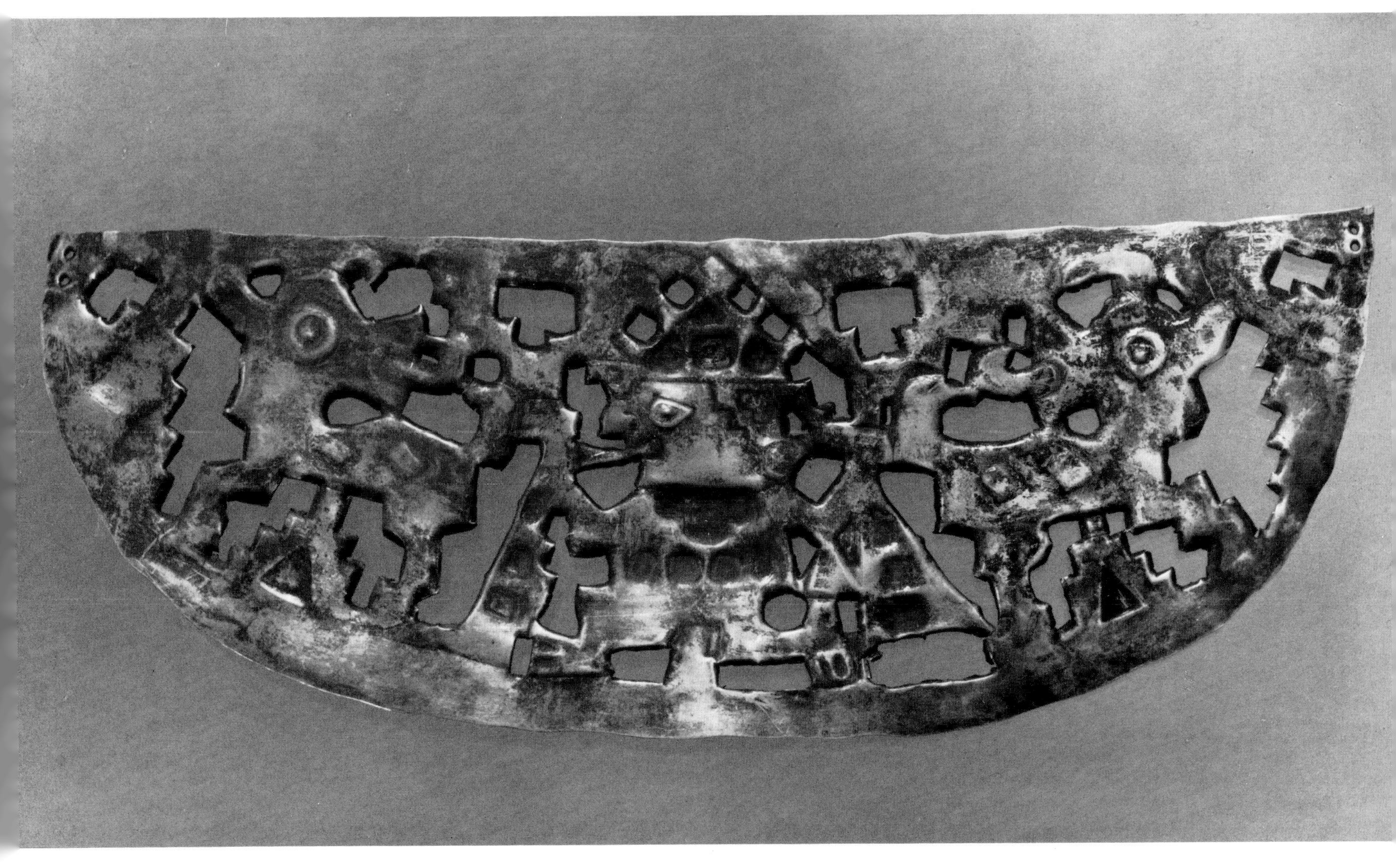

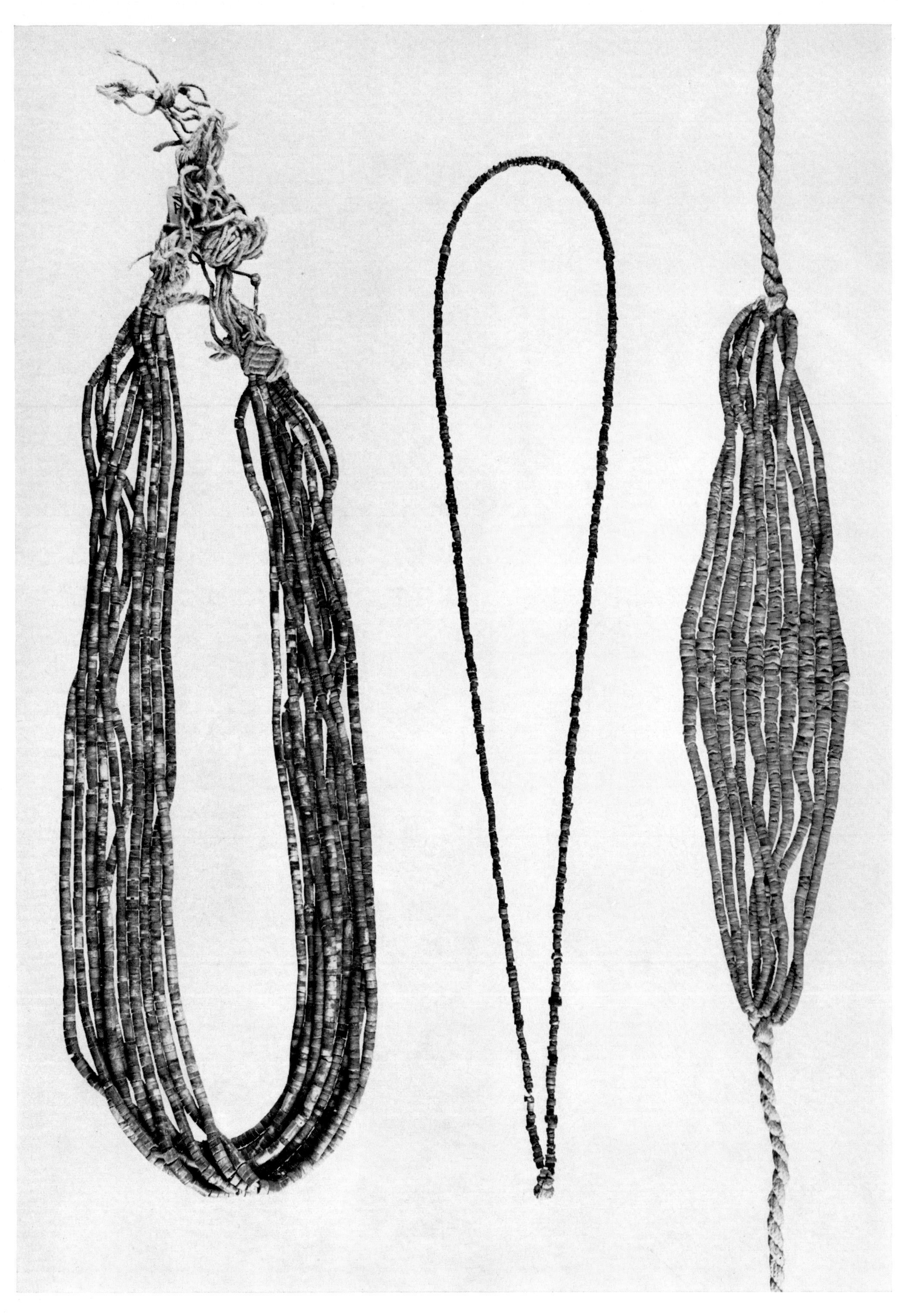

Facing page:
The three necklaces plainly illustrate the level of the ancient Peruvians' goldsmith's art. Modern goldsmiths admire the skillfull craftsmanship, which deserves all the more credit when one bears in mind the primitive nature of their equipment. Collection of Dr. P. Ludwig, Aachen.

Parts of this heavy gold bracelet with ornamental bosses are covered with the typical brownish Peruvian gold patina. Origin unknown. It could date from the Tiahuanaco period, during which the bow first reached the Peruvian coast. It may have been intended primarily as protection against the recoil of the bowstring. Height $6^{1}/_{8}$ ins. Museum für Völkerkunde, Munich.

This gold vessel in the form of a bird, made of several separate pieces, probably came from the north of Peru. Width approx. $7^3/_4$ ins. Weight 156.2 grammes. Collection of Dr. P. Ludwig, Aachen.

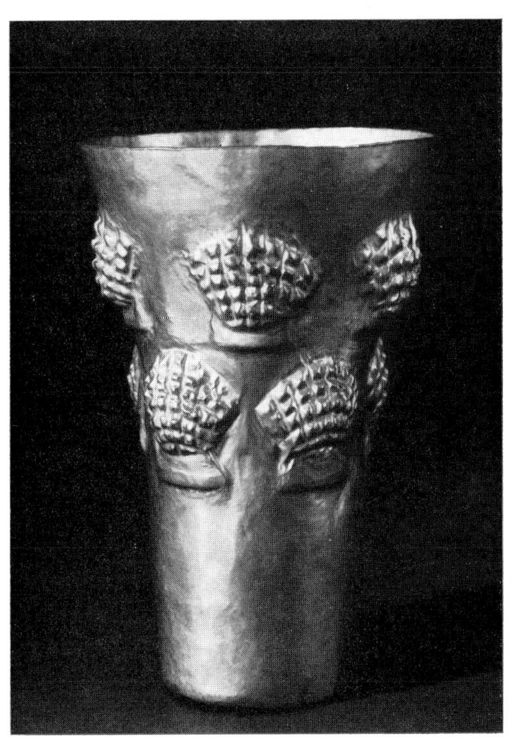

In recent years more than 100 gold beakers are supposed to have been found in the grave of a prince or a priest, that lay at the foot of a group of adobe pyramids, near Ilimo in north Peru. A great find of gold treasure was uncovered in the vicinity some decades earlier, and was partly melted down. Judging by their style, these three beakers come from the same region (Lambayeque province). The figure of a deity, sea shells, and clubs with human heads are depicted in relief. Weight 208 grammes, 194 grammes, 94.6 grammes. Height approx. 9 ins., 6 ins. and $5^3/_8$ ins. Collection of Dr. P. Ludwig, Aachen.

The two gold llama figures are typical of the work of Inca goldsmiths. 15th century. Museum für Völkerkunde, Hamburg.

The mosaic discs, inlaid with pieces of turquoise and seashells, are the fronts of ear-plugs. Diameter $2^3/_8$ ins. and approx. $3^1/_2$ ins. Late Tiahuanaco, 8th–9th centuries A.D. Copacabana, Bolivia. Museum für Völkerkunde, Berlin.

Trade and Transport

Man and the llama were the only pack-animals in ancient Peru, and of the two man was possibly the more important. Accounts vary as to how much a llama used to carry. The maximum weights recorded vary between 66 pounds and 110 pounds, but over shorter distances man can carry more. Moreover llamas were not native to all regions. The llama is the largest of the domestic animals of ancient America, and is happiest in the upper altitudes, where it thrives on certain herbs, in particular the hard ichu grass.

The llama was very rarely ever ridden, and was never used as a draft animal. (The wheel and cart did not exist, and oxen, asses and horses were introduced by the Spaniards.) In ancient times it was probably the same as today, with the male llama carrying small loads, and both men and women also acting as pack-animals. The llamas used for transporting goods covered long distances in caravans, and although they do not have much stamina and therefore have to be changed frequently, they are able to hold out for days on end without water in the bleak mountain *punas*, which no horse or mule could do. The leading male, its ears adorned with red wool threads and tassels, is well aware of its position of honor. It does not have to carry anything, and the others, their loads packed in two woolen saddle bags or in nets, follow him like their lord. Occasionally the entire caravan was festively decked out, and the animals covered in red paint. Men usually carried their loads by a band which went across the chest and back, and went at a running trot. Loads were also wrapped up in pieces of cloth and carried on the back, with the corners of the cloth knotted across the chest. The use of carrying bands across the forehead for carrying loads, which was customary in other parts of ancient America, appears to have been uncommon in ancient Peru.

Litters for personal transportation appear to have always been the privilege of the nobility throughout Peru. This was certainly the case in the Inca empire, when two or more bearers would carry the princes. The litters were open in war, and canopied in times of peace. Spanish chroniclers relate that when they saw the Inca Atahualpa for the first time at the hot baths of the city of Cajamarca, he was borne by more than eighty litterbearers dressed in blue liveries.

Litters of various kinds appear to have existed even in earliest times, either simple carrying devices slung across two poles, enclosed chairs, or hammocks. The Inca litters were enriched with gold and silver fittings.

A magnificent network of streets and roadways facilitated travel across difficult terrain. Hanging bridges spanned rivers and ravines, and rest-houses provided comforts for the traveller.

Transportation by water, on the large inland lakes in the highlands, was by reed boats, like those in use today on Lake Titicaca. They are made up of bundles of reeds bound together, and taper to a point at the bow and stern. The larger reed boats are even fitted out with sails of matting or cloth. On flat reaches they are punted along with poles, that also serve as oars. The largest of the reed *balsas* are up to twenty feet long.

The reed boats used along the coast are much smaller and are always one-man fishing vessels. It appears that in ancient times larger reed *balsas* were also built along the coast. Today they usually consist of only three reed bundles, cleverly cut and arranged in such a way that the pointed bow curved upwards. The boats used at sea are squared off at the stern. Large or small groups of them carry the fishermen miles out into the open sea. They are known as *Caballitos* (little horses), and are steered and driven forwards with thick, split bamboo poles.

Sea-going log rafts of light balsa wood were built for the most part in north Peru and in present-day Ecuador, although fishermen's rafts made of three logs can occasionally be seen in the calm bays of the south. Light balsa wood does not, as incorrectly assumed by some authors, grow only in Ecuador,

Raft of gourd flasks, Chimú, Museum für Völkerkunde, Cologne

but also in the Peruvian forests east of the Andes. The oldest known illustration of a sea-going Ecuador log-raft was published by the Italian, Benzoni, in 1572, and shows two of these craft, each made of three logs, with fishermen in the background. These are still in use in southern Peru and in Ecuador. It is well known that in 1526 Pizarro's pilot, Bartolomé Ruiz met a large sailing *balsa* with twenty men and cargo aboard in Ecuador waters. Later still, Alexander von Humboldt saw log rafts with cabins. The Spanish Conquistadors even saw log rafts on Lake Junin and Lake Titicaca, the two great highland lakes of Peru. Huayna Capac, the next to last reigning Inca, had apparently had them brought there.

Rafts made of gourds and of inflated sealskins were used only in certain areas. These must have been rather unstable.

In Inca times all foreign trade was apparently a state monopoly. There is no detailed information on the subject. Local markets must have been held under Inca rule at which trading between different regions took place, just as in earlier times. The present-day markets, held on different days of the week in certain places, give us some idea of what marketing conditions must have been like in those times. Money was unknown before the arrival of the Spaniards, and trading by barter still occurs in many mountain areas and in some valleys. Certain products such as salt, chili pepper and a kind of copper axe of no practical value were used as a form of money substitute in ancient times. Some of the local markets, linked with certain local saints' days and other church festivals, are famous. Men and women squatting on the ground, with the produce of their fields and gardens displayed for sale in little heaps in front of them, must have been as common a sight in ancient times as they are today. Their wares included ground-nuts, chili peppers, cactus fruits, paltas and other fruits, depending on the region the vendors came from. Valleys with widely varying climates, producing different varieties of fruits, often lie quite close to one another. People try to acquire whatever they lack by barter, and sometimes these transactions are even conducted in complete silence, with the buyer and seller placing their wares alongside each other's, until both are satisfied and each reaches for his share. The wares are spread out on home-woven cloths—corn in various forms, fresh, roasted, boiled or as pop-corn, all in little heaps, fresh potatoes and the potato preserve known as *chuño*, beans, both raw and cooked, ready for immediate consumption. Eating and drinking must certainly have played an important role in the markets of earlier times too. Everywhere there are stalls selling *chicha*, the home brewed maize beer; for the sun beats down, and the air is dry and dusty.

Dried fish and dried mussels from the coast are transported to the highlands and in return dried meat *(charque)* and live sheep are brought to the coast. In some areas frogs and a specially prepared soil are also traded. Somewhere in nearly every market there is a stack of pottery wares which are bartered for field produce.

Obviously, minted money nowadays fulfills a certain function. But even at the present time the ancient customs persist and, as we have said, goods are still bartered at native markets.

Inca woman carrying jug

Litter with four bearers. Fired pottery with polychrome painting. 8th–11th century A.D. Late Tiahuanaco. Height $10^{5}/_{8}$ ins. Private Collection, Basel.

Princes and leaders were carried in litters. The litter-bearers were recruited from certain definite areas. This sculpture was found in the central Peruvian coastland. Fired pottery, painted red and brown on a light background. Height $4^3/_4$ ins. Private Collection, Basel.

Litters were mostly made of wood, and were often decorated with inlay work of precious stones and furnished with gold and silver fittings. Hammock litters are comparatively rare in Peru. Above: pottery model of a hammock litter, painted black and red on grey. Inca period. Central coast of Peru. Museum für Völkerkunde, Berlin.

Four bearers carrying a litter appear on this appliqué design, sewn on to a thin cotton fabric. Size $5^3/_8 \times 6^1/_2$ ins. Chimú style. Museum für Völkerkunde, Berlin.

Left: large, masted reed boats made up of bundles of reeds still sail on Lake Titicaca (10,826 ft. above sea level), as in ancient times.

Right: the reed boats used along the coast today are much smaller than the sailing boats of the highland lakes. They also differ in shape. They are mostly one-man vessels. Pottery model of a reed boat with fishermen. Moche culture. Museum für Völkerkunde, Berlin.

The wooden models of a boat and a log-raft come from north Chile. The canoe, left, from a grave in the Azapa valley, dates from Inca times. The raft, above, comes from the Playa Miller, Arica, and dates from approximately A.D. 1200. Arica Museum (Chile).

Boats of inflated seal-skins were known only in the south. They were still in use on a number of rivers in south Peru in the nineteenth century. The model of this kind of boat, pictured here, comes from the coast of north Chile. After 1000 A.D. Red stone. Museum für Völkerkunde, Hamburg.

Facing page:
This ancient Indian market group consists of individual pottery vessels of the Moche culture. Each figure offers different wares, clothing, animals, etc.

The peanut vendor could easily fit in with the other figures of the market group. Height $9\frac{1}{2}$ ins., likewise the squatting figure, holding a bird. Greyish-black pottery. Lambayeque style. Monheim Collection, Aachen.

Above: the jug on the back of this Inca citizen probably holds maize beer or even water. Water is precious and often has to be carried long distances. In Peru, unlike in ancient Mexico, the method of carrying was more commonly by a band across the chest, rather than by a head-band. Museum für Völkerkunde, Berlin.

Knot-record, the so-called *quipu* which was used for statistical purposes and as a mnemonic aid, and consisted of different colored threads tied together at the top. We have little exact information regarding the places or circumstances in which these were found. Museum für Völkerkunde, Berlin.

It is amazing what heavy loads women could carry. Was it fashion, personal preference, or simply practical experience that determined the choice of the headband rather than the band across the chest for carrying? Left: in the Linden Museum, Stuttgart; below: red and white painted pottery vessel. Height $5^1/_2$ ins. Moche style. British Museum, London.

Right: despite the heavy load on her back, the woman cannot do without the small, woven bag, which she carries over her arm. It may have held her food for the day, a hand spindle, some cotton, and other necessities. Painted, two-color pottery vessel. Moche culture. Museum für Völkerkunde, Berlin.

The llama, the only Peruvian pack animal, originally came from the highlands. However it was brought to the coast to be traded as a sacrificial animal, and for transporting produce. The maximum load a llama can carry is apparently 110 pounds. Right: the contents of the jugs may have been too heavy for the llama, so that it was forced to rest. Painted pottery. Moche culture. Private Collection, Basel.

Below: llamas are not ridden. But occasionally when its master is tired or drunk, he lies down flat on it and lets himself be carried by the animal. Moche culture. Linden Museum, Stuttgart.

Below, right: this is a rare piece. The vessel, in the form of a tribeswoman wearing a head-scarf, with a light pack on her back, has a slightly conical spout. The young llama, led by a rope, is painted on the vessel. Multi-colored painted pottery. Tiahuanaco style from the Nazca region, about A.D. 850. Leyden Museum.

Facing page: ceramics from the upper Santa valley frequently show llamas being led by a rope. The master walks in front, even carrying the tired dog. Recuay style, about A.D. 500. Height approx. 4 ins. British Museum, London.

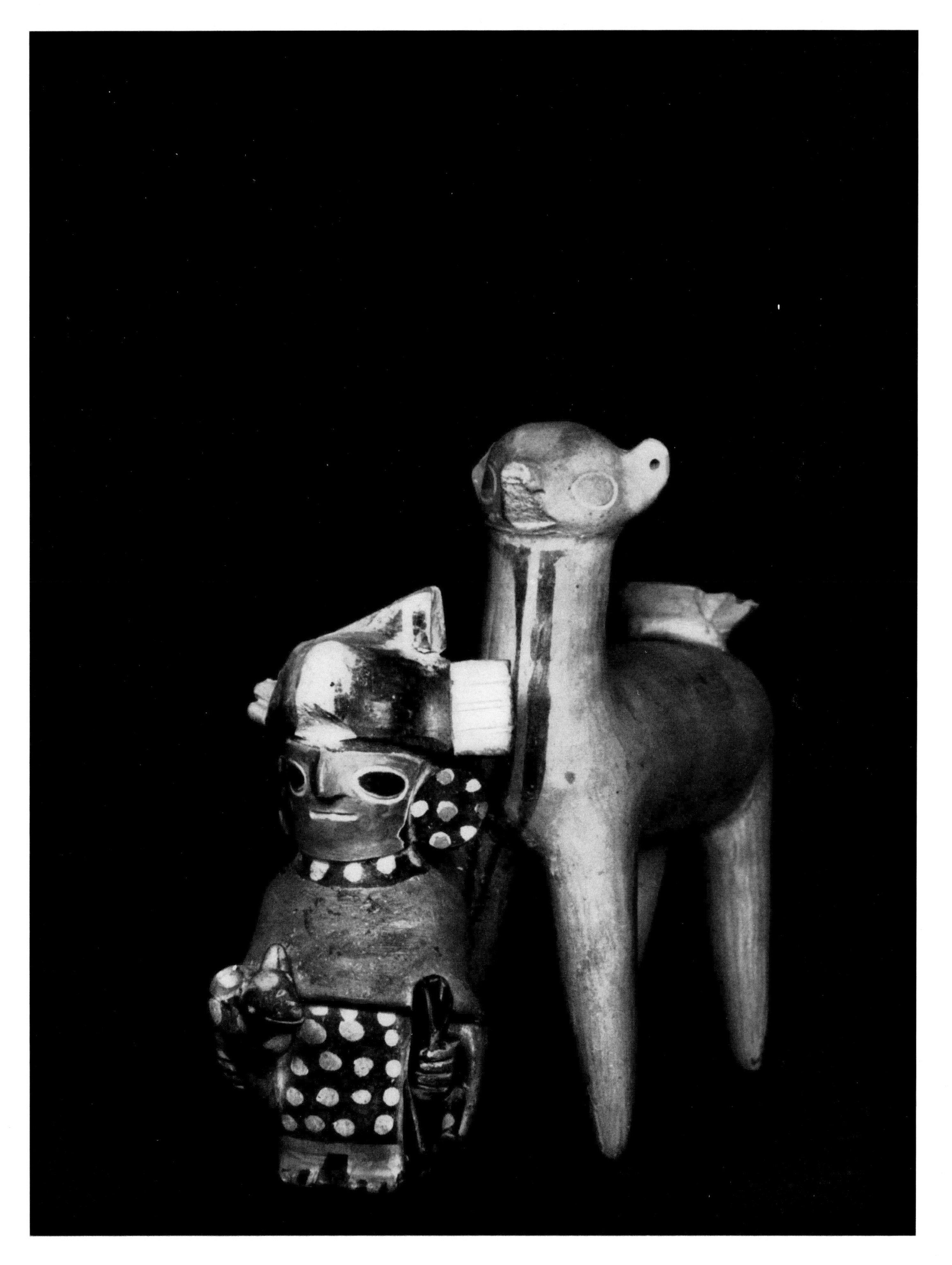

This primitive, stylized sculpture in grey pottery is an archetype of the proud llama with its long, upright neck. Peruvian coast. Period and exact place of origin unknown. Height $4^3/_8$ ins. Museum für Völkerkunde, Vienna.

Music and Dancing

It is surprising that in Peru, as in the whole of ancient America, stringed instruments were quite unknown. The ancient graves in the coastal region of Peru have yielded only percussion and wind instruments, and models of these, which have found their way into the museums of the world.
Some of these ancient instruments are still played today in the Andean highlands, from Colombia in the north, down to Bolivia in the south. The harp, guitar and violin, introduced during the early Spanish colonial period and played by all the village bands, have not been able to drive out the flutes and drums. The music of those Indian bands that perform without harps and fiddles at village feasts must surely come closest to the pentatonic music of their ancestors.
The simple long flutes have from three to six finger-holes. Nowadays one hardly ever sees flutes carved of bone—they are most commonly made of reeds. The pan-pipes, now played chiefly in the Peruvian and Bolivian highlands, are made of five or more reeds bound together. In the highlands of Ecuador, I once saw a really magnificent set of pan-pipes, made from the enormous pinion feathers of the condor. In ancient times pan-pipes were also modelled in clay; they are by no means uncommon, but were probably only intended as funerary gifts. Graves have also yielded trumpets of fired clay, sometimes painted or decorated with figures. Straight trumpets come from the graves of the Nazca valleys, south of Lima, curved ones from northern Peru. A kind of alpenhorn, which I heard years ago in the mountain town of Cajamarca in north Peru, consisted of a reed almost six feet long, with a bell-mouth at the end, made from a gourd. Trumpets made from the shells of giant sea-snails, sometimes modelled in clay, have been found in graves all over the country, and occasionally natives who have stumbled on them while working in the fields or building houses, have begun to play them with religious awe. They signal to each other with them, and at eclipses of the moon they use the harsh sounds of these conches to frighten off the wild beast, which according to their ancient beliefs, threatens to devour the moon. In ancient times the conch trumpet was probably chiefly used in war. Drums were likewise used in times of war. The reed flutes were probably played by young men, to express their unhappiness in love, just as the mountain shepherds do today.

Apart from this, it is likely that ancient music was often connected with religious ritual. Hide drums, covered with llama, deer or sometimes even human skin, provided the rhythm. There were large and small hide drums. Drums made of fired clay have been discovered in graves, but these are comparatively rare. Drums also accompanied religious singing. Dancers held tambourines and rattles, filled with small stones, in their hands. Copper bells and bands threaded with snail shells and seed pods adorned the ankles and thighs of the dancers, who stamped their feet to the rhythm.

The sound of music is an invitation to the dance; there is no dancing without music. Most of the ancient Peruvian dances, probably all, were of a ritual nature, handed down by tradition. There were dances for men and dances for women, and some for both to perform together.

Father Bernabé Cobo (1653) has left us with some detailed information about some of the dances of the Inca period. He saw the Indians still dancing their ancient dances in the Inca capital, Cuzco, after the conquest, and lists these dances by name. There was, then, a kind of jumping dance performed only by men. They wore masks and were dressed up as animals. Another dance, in which the women participated, was accompanied by a musical instrument fashioned out of a deer's head. The faces of the women were painted. Father Cobo relates that there was one dance that imitated the cultivation of the soil, in which the dancers held agricultural implements. There was a war dance that was performed on particularly important occasions. A kind of slow reel, performed only

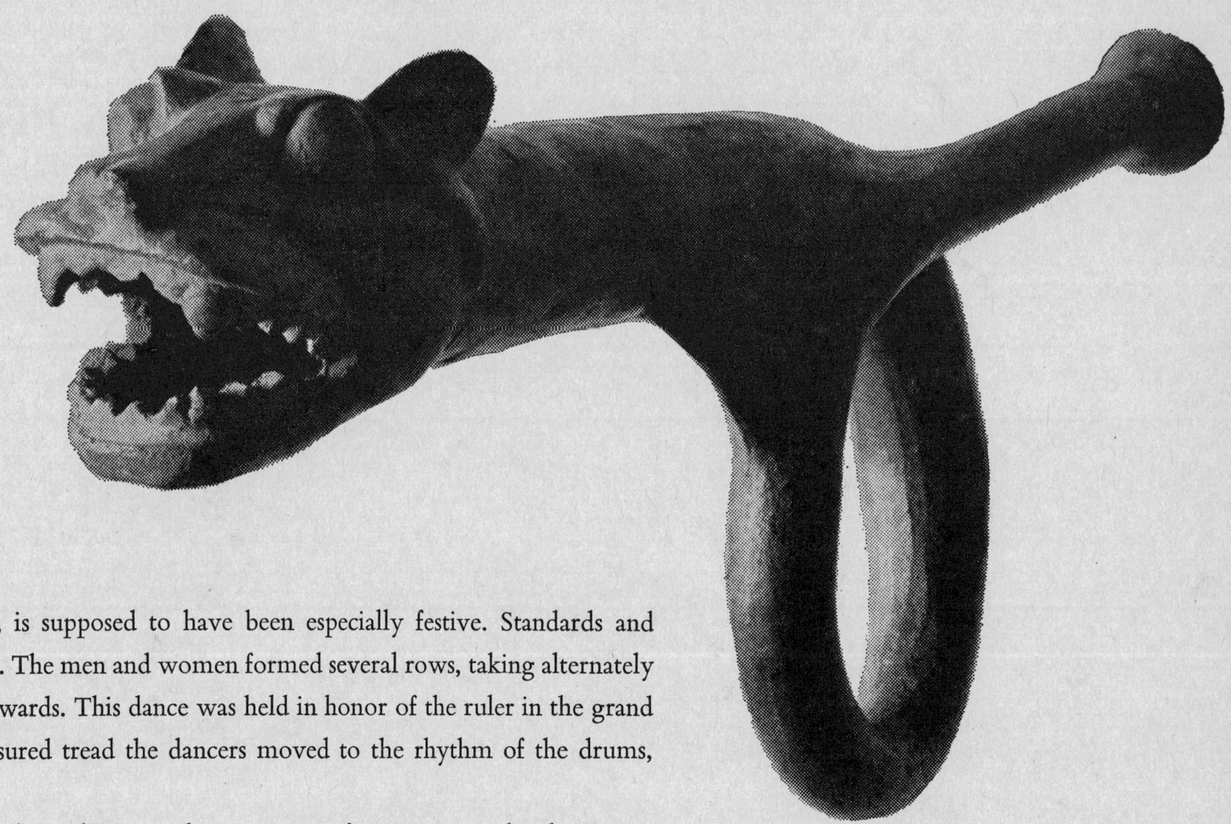

Pottery trumpet, ending in the form of the head of a wild beast. Moche. Private Collection, Zürich

by members of the reigning family, is supposed to have been especially festive. Standards and emblems of the ruler were borne aloft. The men and women formed several rows, taking alternately two steps forwards and one step backwards. This dance was held in honor of the ruler in the grand square in Cuzco. With solemn, measured tread the dancers moved to the rhythm of the drums, approaching the throne of the Inca.

Whereas we are fairly well informed about the musical instruments of ancient times by the instruments and models of musicians discovered in graves, representations of dances and dancers are far less frequent.

As far as the music itself is concerned, musical scholars are of the opinion that sounds and rhythms from pre-Spanish times persist in contemporary folk music. Further detailed research is necessary before all the original content disappears.

A dancing couple, man and woman, playing the flute and drum and shaking bells. These beautifully worked figurines came from the region of Lambayeque in the northern coastal area of Peru. Date uncertain but definitely pre-Inca. Museum für Völkerkunde, Hamburg.

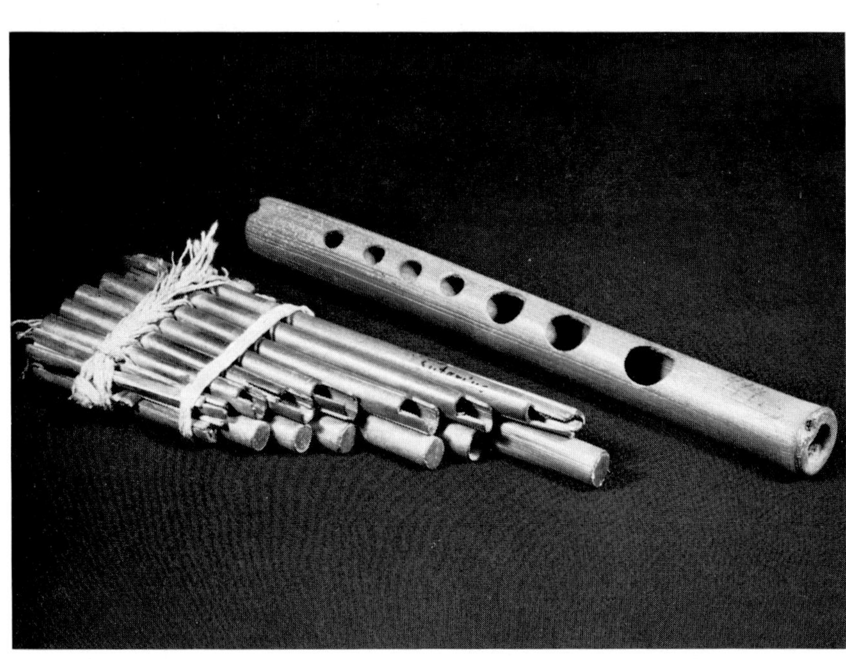

Decorated, simple curved trumpets of fired pottery are found in the northern coastal valleys. In the Nazca region there are trumpets with very fine painted decorations. One instrument that survives to this day is the pan-pipes, which appear in different sizes and are made up of varying numbers of reeds.

Facing page:
Trumpet in the form of a warrior with nose ornament. Reddish pottery. $12^5/_8$ ins. British Museum, London.

Right: a dancer in full ceremonial attire, including a tall helmet, and ear ornaments, playing a tambourine. Gold figure from the region of Lambayeque (north Peru). Height $3^1/_2$ ins. Museum für Völkerkunde, Hamburg.

Below: pan-pipes and simple reed flute. Approx. 6 ins. and 8 ins. Linden Museum, Stuttgart.

Above: the man playing the pan-pipes in a reclining position is the work of a potter from the Chimú kingdom on the north coast. Black pottery. 13th–15th centuries. Width $9^7/_8$ ins. Museum für Völkerkunde, Berlin.

Right: trumpets in the form of a warrior and a man playing pan-pipes. Reddish pottery. $12^1/_5$ ins. Moche culture, approx. 500 A.D. Linden Museum Stuttgart, and British Museum, London.

Flutes are made of reed, pottery or metal. These two are made from human bone, possibly from the arm of a slain enemy. Length $7^{9}/_{10}$ ins. and $8^{3}/_{10}$ ins. Linden Museum, Stuttgart.

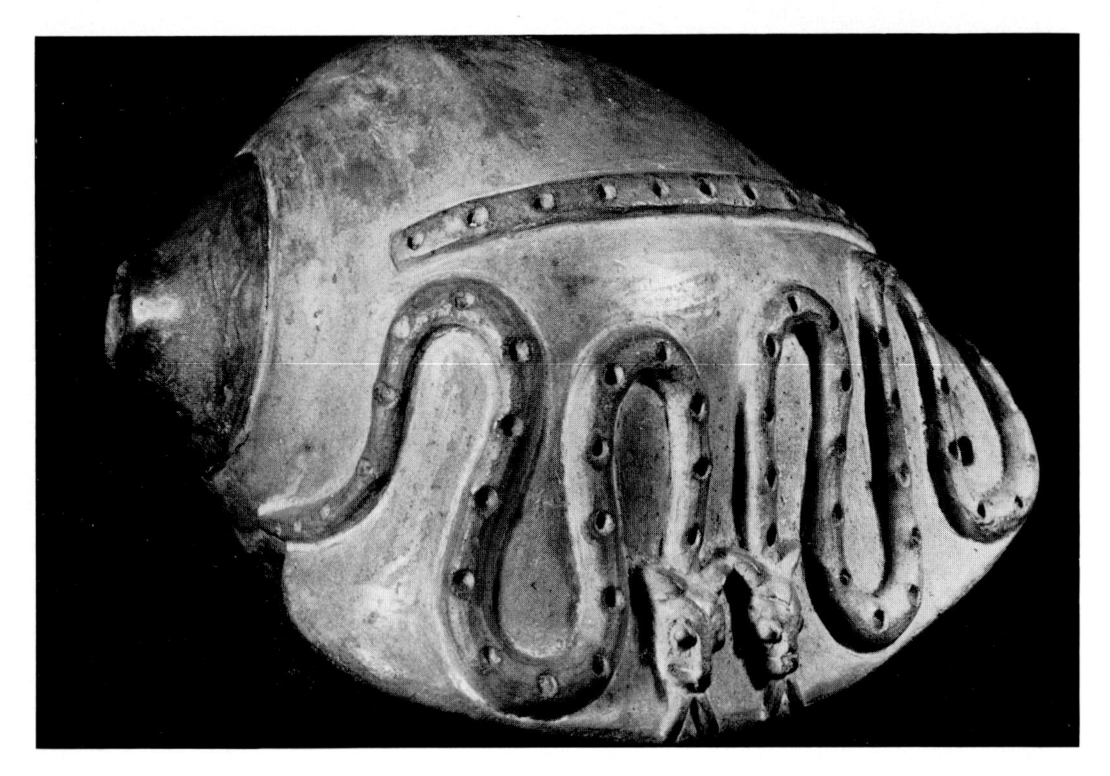

In remote areas conch trumpets are still played today on special occasions. Left: model of a conch trumpet. Brown painted on off-white pottery. Snake sculptured in relief. Width $8^{7}/_{8}$ ins. Early Moche culture. Linden Museum, Stuttgart.

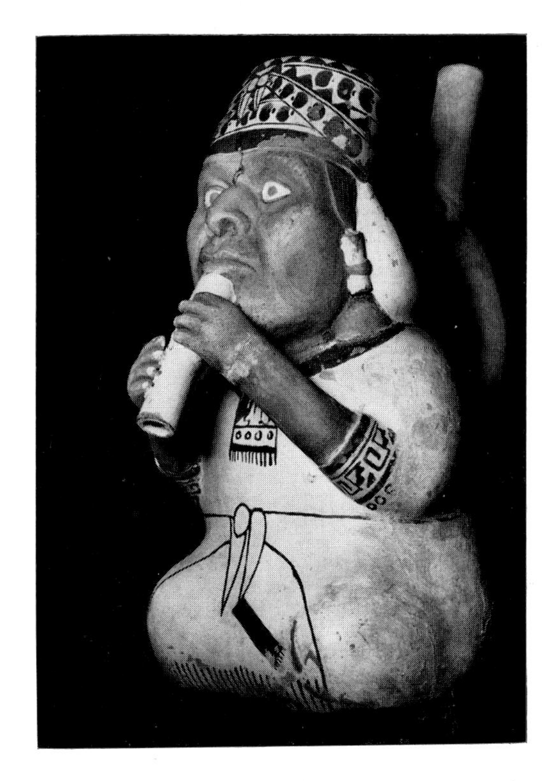

Percussion instruments and rattles of various types, shapes and sizes were known throughout the whole of Peru. The squatting man (above left) is striking a hide drum. Figure on top of pottery vessel. Chimú. Museum für Völkerkunde, Berlin.

Above, center: the two halves of a large seashell could be used as a kind of cymbals. Unusual piece in dark pottery, showing traces of paint. Chimú. Museum für Völkerkunde, Hamburg.

Above, right: squatting flute-player in bright red pottery. Red paint on a white wash. Height $12^1/_5$ ins. Moche culture. British Museum, London. There are many portrayals of deformed musicians, such as the man playing the hand-drum (below, left). Height $4^5/_8$ ins. Linden Museum, Stuttgart.

Below, center: man blowing a conch trumpet, in brownish-grey pottery. Height approx. 7 ins. Moche culture. H. G. Monheim Collection, Aachen.

Below, right: kneeling musician playing three instruments. The main instrument is the pottery drum, accompanied by pan-pipes and trumpet. Pottery vessel with polychrome painting. Late Nazca, about A.D. 1000. Height $7^3/_4$ ins. Private Collection, Zürich.

This rare portrayal of a round-dance with tambourines was discovered by the author on a rock-drawing in Toro Muerto (Majes valley, south Peru).

Above right: dancers in rich, cult apparel appear on the sumptuous, multi-colored embroidered shrouds found at Paracas. Paracas necropolis, 1st century B.C. Museo Nacional, Lima.

Throughout the whole of ancient America, music and dancing were accompanied by rattling instruments of various kinds. Wooden rattles decorated with figures, from the north coast of Peru. Private Collection, Zürich, and Museum für Völkerkunde, Basel.

Facing page; above: wooden rattling stick filled with small pebbles. Private Collection, Zürich.

Right: man playing pan-pipes, with llama. Red and black painted on a light background. Recuay style. Height $8^1/_4$ ins. Museum für Völkerkunde, Berlin.

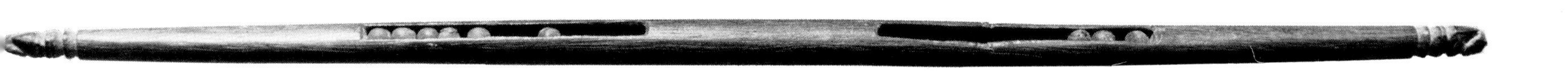

Bearers carrying military bells, and pan-pipe players. Part of a musical procession. Vase painting, reddish-brown on an ivory-colored background. Upper Chicama valley, north Peru. Museo Nacional, Lima.

In political terms, the Inca state represents a peak of achievement in the cultural history of ancient America. Opinion is divided about the socialism of the Inca state, if socialism is the right word. Some authors go so far as to talk of communism, whereas the Peruvian historical philosopher and social historian, Haya de la Torre maintains that, of all the state systems that have existed in the world, the Inca state was the closest approximation to Plato's concept of the state. The facts are that the Inca empire lasted for not quite a hundred years, and the American scholar, John Howard Rowe, is absolutely right when he asserts that the amazing speed with which the Spaniards effected their conquest of the Inca empire is a reflection of the fundamental weakness of that imperial system. The Inca people were a flock without a shepherd, once their emperor had been taken.

The State and the Family

Walter Krickeberg (see Appendix), on the other hand, is of the opinion that the Inca state, despite its unified and centralized character, was by no means an original creation. The Inca state, according to Krickeberg, was not the great socialist state that some "democratic Utopians" would have us believe, but the end result of a long process of evolution from ancient American forms of society. The keen political sense and insight of the Incas did, in fact, incorporate all kinds of long-established social institutions into its governmental system and perfected them to the utmost degree.

As the village societies with their intense community spirit produced such extraordinary achievements by their joint enterprises, the Incas did not dream of dissolving them. On the contrary, this system was to the advantage of the state as a whole. The severe laws of the Incas did, however, put an end to the struggles between individual village communities over water rights and the ownership of herds. The obligation to work was imposed like a levy by the Inca rulers throughout the entire state. They were the divine sovereigns who granted special privileges to the nobility in the administration of the state, but also saw to it that even the aged and the sick never went hungry. "Father of the poor" was one of the laudatory names of the Inca. Bad harvests no longer meant privation. Store-houses erected in every part of the land were full of provisions. Father Cobo gives a graphic description of these store-houses: "The stores that were kept in them consisted of all the things that the people would pay as taxes—enormous amounts of corn, quinoa grain, potato preserve and fresh vegetables. There was an abundance of dried llama, deer, and vicuna meat, clothing made from various materials—wool, cotton and feathers, as well as sandals, called *Ojotas*. Our men found the store-houses filled with all these things." The Father goes on to relate how by force of long-established habit the Indians continued to collect their field produce in these warehouses for the Inca and the deities, even after the arrival of the Spaniards, in the belief that the day would come when they would have to settle their accounts with the Inca. This proved to be of great benefit to the Spaniards during the warring feuds that broke out after the conquest. Bernabé Cobo writes: "When President Pedro de la Gasca moved up the Jauja valley in pursuit of Gonzalo Pizarro and had to remain there for seven months, his soldiers did not go short of food during the whole of this time. For the warehouses were piled high with the harvests of many years. Even if the demand had been much greater the warehouses in the valleys would still not have been exhausted."

Under the Incas, the whole empire was divided up into four major sections, all converging at Cuzco, the capital, which was not merely the geographical center of the *Tahuantinsuyu*, the "Land of the Four Quarters." The whole of it was controlled by officials of varying ranks. The science of statistics was highly developed. Everything was counted—not merely people, for example, in the recruiting of manpower for public works such as the construction of irrigation canals, agricultural terraces and roads, but also livestock and all commodities. It is probably no exaggeration when Baudin, the French sociologist, claims that everything was counted "from the game killed at hunts down to

Young Inca with conch trumpet, stone club and sling

the sling-stones deposited in the state magazines." The organization was quite brilliant, extending as it did to the minutest details, dividing the populace into age groups, into bodies of ten thousand, one thousand, five hundred and one hundred; the smallest unit consisted of ten men.

Inca rule only impinged on family life insofar that certain age groups were recruited for the army and for public works, and the most beautiful girls were selected at a tender age for temple service and to satisfy the personal demands of the emperor. There were only certain restrictions that governed the starting of a family. Marriage between blood relations was the privilege of the nobility. Sister marriage, the subject of some controversy, was not in fact made obligatory for the emperor until the reign of the tenth Inca, Tupac Yupanqui, and was intended to guarantee purity of blood. In addition, the emperor had a harem of concubines at his disposal, but this in no way affected the position of the chief wife. For economic reasons alone, polygamy was rarely ever feasible for the common people.

The young wife would settle into the house of the husband. Adultery could lead to a death penalty. Children were welcomed as a potential labor force. According to Garcilaso they were strictly brought up and physically hardened at a very early age, although they were seldom punished.

All this applies to the time of the empire and to the central province of the Inca empire. We know little about family life in earlier times or in other parts of ancient Peru, except that in a number of provinces conditions of matriarchy prevailed. Thus, when the Spaniards entered the land, they encountered female leaders, too.

Garcilaso relates, moreover, that even the wives of the Inca rulers used to suckle their own infants. The sixth emperor, Inca Roca, already appears to have founded schools in Cuzco. Admittedly these were only for the young aristocrats and provided instruction in the state religion, oratory, the history of the ruling dynasty, the Inca calendar, the keeping of knot-records *(quipu)*, and, not least, the art of warfare. Other children began at a very early age, as they still do today, to learn from their parents and from older children how to make themselves useful. Each age group had its specific tasks. We know they had dolls and tops as toys. Races were held for boys in Inca times. The use of the sling was learned at an early age.

Domestic animals were an integral part of the family, and there was probably not a house without some pets. The Andean people may pride themselves on having raised the largest variety of plants in ancient America, as well as on having domesticated the most animals.

Whereas in earlier times feuds had raged between minor population groups, between individual village communities, and between the inhabitants of entire valleys over the ownership of livestock and land and water rights, sometimes even involving plunder and rape, in Inca times war was exclusively a state affair. Men of a certain age group were obliged to do military service, just as in peace time they had to contribute to public works. The neighbors left at home would tend the fields of a departed warrior as a matter of course, so that no family ever had to suffer hardship. Warriors who displayed outstanding courage would be rewarded with clothing and jewelry, and sometimes even with women. Distinction in war was the only way in which the common man could advance himself socially.

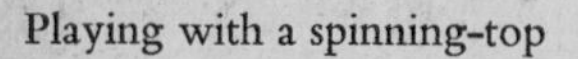

Playing with a spinning-top

Inca prince and his wives in penitence

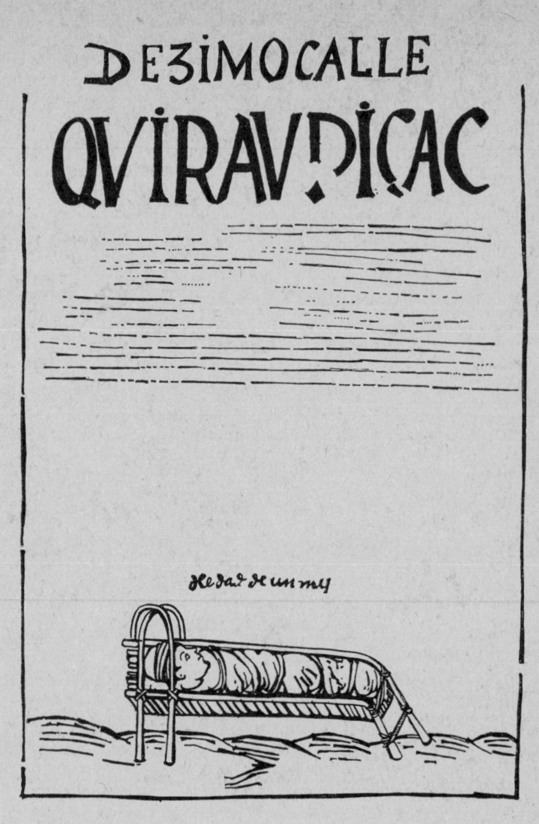

Child's cradle

Helmets of wood or plaited cane and quilted cotton armor were used for protection. There were round and long shields of wood and hide. The chief offensive weapon used in hand-to-hand combat was a club with a stone head, whose shape varied according to the period and region of origin. In Inca times the club heads were ring and star-shaped and made of stone, copper or bronze. There were also sword-shaped clubs made from the hardwood of the Chonta palm and metal halberd-like battle-axes. Bows and arrows were comparatively rare in the Andean region, while the far older throwing-spears were still used by a few of the Inca warrior groups. The most important missile weapons were still slings and bolas, the weapons of shepherds and huntsmen.

It was not in arms alone that the Incas were superior to the peoples they conquered. At the height of their power, there were many instances of peaceful conquest effected by exemplary organization and administration, and by the prestige of their ruler.

The cardinal moral laws imposed on the people were quite simple: Do not steal, do not lie, do not idle. The command to work was perhaps the most important, and the most modern.

The Spaniards may have prided themselves on bringing certain personal liberties to the former subjects of the Inca, such as the acquisition of property, which they could never have owned under Inca rule, and the freedom to settle wherever they chose. But the Indians thought otherwise. They knew that they had exchanged the paternal care, justice and strength of their ruler, whom they worshipped as their god, for the arbitrary rule of their liberators, who, despite the introduction of good Spanish laws, often exploited them shamelessly, and made no provision for illness and old age, as in former times.

Children's toys were sometimes placed in their graves. Sometimes it is hard to tell whether these were actually toys or amulets. Three cloth dolls. H. G. Monheim Collection, Aachen.

The Moche people did not shrink from portraying any aspect of human life. Above: the birth of a child is portrayed with straight-forward realism. Midwives assist the birth. Group in reddish pottery. Museum für Völkerkunde, Berlin. Right: mother and child. Pottery vessel. Height $7\frac{1}{2}$ ins. Moche culture. Linden Museum, Stuttgart.

This seemingly primitive pottery sculpture of a mother suckling her child belongs to the beginnings of the Moche culture. A rare piece from the neighborhood of Piura (north Peru). Fired pottery with reddish wash. Height $6^1/_2$ ins. Collection of Dr. P. Ludwig, Aachen. These highly stylized pottery figurines painted light brown and black may have been dolls or idols. Typical Nazca style. Actual size. Monheim Collection, Aachen.

Certain portrayals in ancient Peruvian art have been quite unjustifiably described as pornographic. Left: the husband and wife asleep with their child are shown in a perfectly natural way. Group of figures on a pottery vessel painted white and red. Height approx. 6 ins. Moche culture. Collection of Dr. P. Ludwig, Aachen.

The family group beneath a dish of fine black pottery, supported by caryatids is a priceless ceramic from a later date. Chimú culture. Private Collection, Basel.

Facing page: polygamy was regarded as perfectly natural in ancient Peru, if the man could afford several wives. It was not until the time of Inca rule that polygamy was restricted to the nobility. The last of the Incas is supposed to have had some two hundred wives apart from his chief-wife, for which the Spaniards severely condemned him. On this pottery vessel from the upper Santa valley, a chieftain is pictured with his wives. Different shades of red painted on a light background. Height 8¼ ins. Collection of Dr. P. Ludwig, Aachen.

The numerous portrayals of warriors, finds of weapons, and the dressed heads of slain enemies, all seem to indicate that warlike activities increased with the formation of distinct social groups. The cult of mummifying the heads of slain warriors, which were thought to possess magic powers, reached its peak in the Nazca and Ica valleys. This richly painted pottery figure shows a Nazca warrior with a trophy head, or possibly a war deity with a mask. Height 12 ins. Early Nazca culture, about 2000 years old. H. G. Monheim Collection, Aachen.

Above: club-head in the shape of a six-pointed star. Pale, polished stone. Chavin culture. 1st or 2nd century B.C.

From earliest times clubs of various shapes were commonly used as weapons. Right: club-heads of red and black stone, decorated with wild animals, incrusted with mussel shells. Museum für Völkerkunde, Berlin. Below: warrior figures from different areas. Left: kneeling warrior with shield, helmet and club. Height $9^1/_2$ ins. Black pottery, Moche culture. Linden Museum, Stuttgart. Right: warrior armed with short club and shield. Upper Santa valley. About A.D. 500. Painted black and red on a pale background. Museum für Völkerkunde, Berlin.

Warrior with clubs, relief on a pottery flask, made from a mould, from one of the northern coastal valleys. Height $12^{1}/_{5}$ ins. Moche culture, Linden Museum, Stuttgart. Stone club-head in the shape of a star into which a wooden handle was inserted. Actual size. Private Collection, Zürich. Facing page: captives used to have their clothing taken away. Naked captive with hands tied behind his back. Reddish-brown pottery. Vicús, before the birth of Christ. Collection of Dr. P. Ludwig, Aachen.

The sick were treated with herbal juices, which were often quite effective, and by the power of suggestion of the healer, who also performed magic, by placing hands on the body, and by massage. Group on a painted pottery vessel. Height approx. 8 ins. Moche culture. Museum für Völkerkunde, Berlin.

Mummified woman with doll. Instances of artificial mummification are very rare. In most cases the process was effected by the dryness of the desert sand. Central coast of Peru 13th–14th century A.D. Museum für Völkerkunde, Hamburg.

Domestic animals such as the llama and the guinea-pig were a part of the family. Llamas were often lovingly decked out. This spotted, reclining llama has a special significance on account of its design. There is a legend in which a spotted llama appears as a constellation in the sky. Tiahuanaco period, style of the Nazca valleys. Painted pottery. Width approx. $11^1/_2$ ins. Museum für Völkerkunde, Munich.

The Human Face

On the whole, ancient Peruvian artists tended to portray the human face in preference to the body. The exception to this general trend is in vase-painting. Here the faces are more or less stylized and are always shown in profile. Jewelry and headdress, always drawn with great care, are all that distinguish one head from another. The exaggerated length of their canine teeth, make the faces of demons instantly recognizable. Fleshless noses, toothless mouths and circular eyes distinguish the dead from the living. On the other hand, the portrayal of human bodies in movement is surprisingly lifelike—running or dancing legs, poised arms and hands, club-swinging warriors, or huntsmen, their arms drawn back to launch their throwing-spears. In nearly every group at least one of the heads is shown looking back. Frequently, the figures and faces in a group are turned towards one another, but never in a symmetrical arrangement. The relative proportions of heads and bodies are fairly accurately preserved.

All this applies to the vase painting of the Moche people, also known as the Mochica, who inhabited the river valleys in the northern coastal region of Peru in the early centuries after Christ. There they constructed irrigation works and built pyramids of adobe bricks. The name, Moche, derives from a place in the vicinity of one of the largest temple pyramids in Peru, which has survived for almost two thousand years, and is known as the Sun Pyramid, although we do not know why.

Most of the two-colored vase paintings depict scenes of war and peace, hunting, paying homage, running races, inspired by myths that are unknown to us. However, they tell us far less about the

Mummy mask, painted wood, height 11 1/2 ins. Linden Museum, Stuttgart.

human face than the pottery sculptures by the same people. These attempt realistic portrayals of individual human faces. It is interesting that sculptures preceded painting in the portrayal of man. Sculptures of the human body and face in stone or fired clay already appeared in the pre-Moche cultures. No wooden figures have survived from this early period, but there are a few demon faces in bone and in gold.

Unlike the art of the Old World, the unnatural proportions of body and head in the portrayals of men persist even in the sculpture of later periods.

The positions of the figure are not at all stiff or stylized. They are shown standing, kneeling, sitting and squatting, with legs straight or folded under. The assumption of some authors that the "Turkish squatting" pose is of Asiatic or even Oriental origin is completely unfounded.

No other cultural region in the world has produced as many sculptures quite apart from the sculptured masks depicting the human head, detached from the body, and often even without a neck. The outer wall of the main temple at Chavin de Huantar (about the time of the birth of Christ) has stone tenon heads let into the masonry either for decoration or as protective talismans. Their circular eyes, snake emblems and fanged teeth place them in the world of demons.

True portrait heads do not appear until Moche ceramic art. They are thought to represent secular and religious dignitaries. This seems more likely than another theory which suggests that these sculptures were portraits of the dead in whose graves they were found. The mere fact that the same heads not only appear in different graves in one and the same valley, but also in several river valley oases separated from one another by great stretches of desert, seems to contradict this unlikely hypothesis. These ceramic heads were cast in moulds and all show exactly the same features; their only variation is in the way they were painted, but they must all portray the same persons. Most probably these were certain highly regarded personalities, whose heads were thought to possess beneficial powers and were consequently portrayed and used as funerary gifts. Similar motivation prompted the ancient Peruvians to place the actual heads of enemies into some graves as an effective magic charm and a valuable funerary gift.

However, there is no doubt that individual portraits were made. The persons portrayed display quite distinct types and characters. Ethnic variations in the individual faces are occasionally so striking that some imaginative authors have been prompted to speak of different races—Indian, negro and white. Whereas it is quite possible that the Moche people was composed of different anthropological groups, there can be no question of black and white. They were all Indians, who are by no means a homogenous racial type.

The emphasis on the eyes in the Mochica portrait heads is quite striking. Their deep expression often dominates the entire face. The dark pupils are set against a pale background. They appear to gaze into the distance or give the impression of calm preoccupation. This impression may be intensified by the way in which the eyes are turned slightly inwards, but not enough to make them actually squint. The lower and upper lids are mostly very delicately modelled, as are the mouth and the flaring nostrils. The mouths express pride and thoughtfulness, silent mourning and sometimes brutality.

The precursors of the Mochica modelled human heads free-hand, without using moulds. Sometimes there is a secretive quality flickering over their features. The coffee bean-shaped eyes in these faces sometimes give them the blank expressions of the dead or the sleeping. The noses always seem to follow a certain pattern, as does the straight line of the mouth. But there are exceptional instances where the features familiar in the later portraits already appear in early times, with their immense eyes that dominate the face.

Stone head of a warrior, north Peruvian highlands. Height 8 $^{1}/_{4}$ ins. Museo Nacional, Lima.

Pottery vessel in the form of a multi-colored, painted head. Nazca culture Private Collection, Darmstadt.

It is curious that all these heads were intended as drinking vessels for the living and the dead. The stirrup spout, with which most of these portrait vessels are furnished, occasionally spoils the artistic effect, especially for those unaccustomed to this unusual feature.

Stone masks are comparatively rare in the area of greater Peru, far more rare than in Mexico, and so are ceramic masks. Wooden masks are painted, with the eyes usually made of a different material, often of mussel shells, but also of sheet-copper. These wooden masks were placed on mummy bundles, and in accordance with their function, they rarely have individual features. Magnificent masks of embossed gold plate may have served the same purpose as the wooden ones. Red pigment, the color of blood, often covers part of the mask face. Similarly only a few of these gold masks have detailed features. They are shrouded in the mystery of death.

Stone statues, which are found chiefly in the highland region, are hierarchically austere. The form of the face is of secondary importance. There are, however, some noteworthy exceptions within the Tiahuanaco culture, which spread all through the land. Besides the stone images which appear to be of a religious nature, there are also some unusually lifelike faces in stone and in fired clay.

In the Tiahuanaco period large painted ceramic faces occur in the Nazca valleys, and with their enormous eyes they would seem to derive from mythical sources. We do not know whether they were meant to be humans or deities. Unusual portrait vessels with winged eyes, dating from an earlier period, have been found in the same region. Ubbelohde-Doering calls them the eyes of dead souls.

The portrayal of the human face was apparently of little significance at the time of the Inca empire. At this time the heads of gold and ceramic figures with stiff and lifeless bodies always bear the same, somewhat monotonous features. The large wooden goblets in rich, resin colors, often decorated with pictorial scenes, do not come from graves, but have been handed down from one generation to the next. They probably all date from colonial times. These goblets are known as *kerus*, and the finest of them, showing figures in Inca dress, date only from the time of the great Indian rising in the 18th century, as has been pointed out by the eminent American scholar John H. Rowe.

Obviously some of the Inca portrait vessels of a similar nature which were used for drink-offerings, must be older. The very stiffness of the huge-eyed faces seems to radiate mystical secrecy. The Inca rulers were deities in human form. Their mummies were kept in the Sun Temple at Cuzco. These vessels were portraits of deities, whose faces were covered by gold masks. Enthroned beneath feathered baldachins, they were carried up to a plain east of the royal city for the Sun Feast.

There is less stylization in this pottery head from Vicús, Department Piira. Despite the primitive technique, this is quite clearly recognizable as a certain North Peruvian tribal type. Brown pottery with traces of negative painting. Height 10¼ ins. Vicús style. Before the birth of Christ. Private Collection, Zürich.

Replicas of portrait heads, made from moulds, have been found in a number of graves, often in different river valleys, which suggests that these were portraits of revered princes or priests, whose magic powers were intended to protect the dead. Portrait head with ear-plugs. Height $8^5/_8$ ins. Painted pottery from the peak period of the northern river valley oases, about A.D. 500. Museum für Völkerkunde, Berlin.

This realistic portrait head is in the unmistakable style of the Moche culture. It is part of a complete figure. Private Collection, Darmstadt.

There is nothing of the portrait in this painted and carved wooden beaker. It was used as a container for sacrificial libations. Height approx. 11 ins. Inca period, Museo de la Universidad, Arequipa.

Head of a potter figure, monochrome. Private Collection, Darmstadt.

There are certain kinds of heads from the Nazca and Ica valleys that are heavily stylized. Ubbelohde-Doering speaks of "dead eyes," and takes these heads for portrayals of dead souls. An outstanding, particularly fine piece. Height over 12 ins. Private Collection, Frankfurt.

The Moche artists were masters of the portrait. Portrait-head with forelock and earrings. Height $5^1/_8$ ins. British Museum, London.

The features of some portrait-heads seem quite un-Indian, and could almost be those on the statues of Western mediaeval princes.

Head of a prince, with nose ornament—possibly a sign of caste. Pale pottery, painted in two colors. Height approx. 10 ins. Linden Museum, Stuttgart.

Right: portrait-like head of a pottery figure, with nose ornament and pendant ear-adornments. The nose ornament is not pottery, but real silver. Museum für Völkerkunde, Berlin.

Facing page: portrait-head with Mongolian features. The Moche people included the most varied racial types. Museum für Völkerkunde, Berlin.

Facing page: squatting woman with peasant features. Huacho region, north of Lima. Reddish pottery. Linden Museum, Stuttgart.

On the whole Peruvian stone sculpture did not attain the perfection of the ancient Mexican works. Yet there are quite a number of stone figures, especially those from the Peruvian-Bolivian Altiplano by Lake Titicaca, which by their concentration on the most essential lines of the human body and face, attain an impressive simplicity.

Below: stone head of an Inca prince, identifiable by the fringe on the forehead. 14th or 15th century. Height 15 ins. Museum für Völkerkunde, Munich.

Above right: early pottery figure, painted and incised. Brown pottery. About 2000 years old, possibly more. The cap-like head covering is typical of the Vicús style. Private Collection, Zürich.

Below, right: standing figure of hard, volcanic stone. Pucará style, about 2000 years old, possibly more. Puno (south Peru). Museo Nacional, Lima.

The Moche potters had a striking predilection for depicting faces marked by disease. Above, left: portrait of a one-eyed man. Height approx. 11 ins. British Museum, London.

Above, right: portrait-head with artificial nose-piece, like the jade ones, for example, common to the Maya priest-princes. Ivory and reddish-brown painted pottery. Height 10$^1/_4$ ins. Collection of Dr. P. Ludwig, Aachen.

Above, center: face disfigured by disease. Portrait-head painted in two colors. Height 10$^1/_4$ ins. Linden Museum, Stuttgart.

Below, left: portrait-head with facial paralysis, set on to a pottery vessel. Red paint on a pale background. Height 11$^5/_8$ ins. University Museum, Trujillo.
Center: portrait-head in bright red pottery. Height 5$^1/_2$ ins. Museum für Völkerkunde, Berlin.
Below, right: head of an old man, with tattooed face. Linden Museum, Stuttgart.

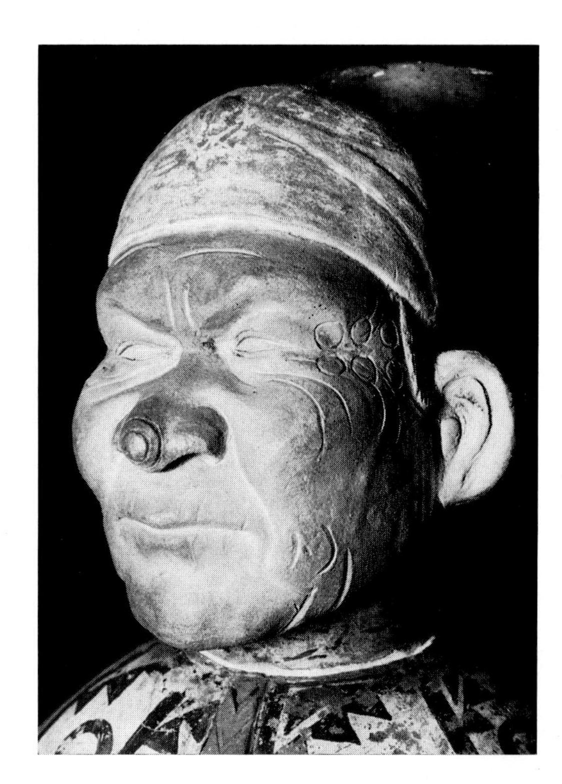

Old woman with a surly expression. Reddish pottery with a pale wash. Moche style. Museum für Völkerkunde, Berlin.

Mask with protruding tongue. Chavin style from the northern coastal region. Before the birth of Christ. Private Collection, Frankfurt.

The Question of Writing

The imperial tongue of the Incas, which is still spoken today by millions of people, possesses a word which may be roughly translated as "writing." In Spanish it is spelled "quilca," and pronounced "kilka." Its meaning is more or less equivalent to "pictorial notation." A more accurate translation has not been found to the present day. However, the mere existence of the word proves that at the time when the Spaniards arrived the Peruvians did have some concept of what we call writing.

In 1560, only 28 years after the arrival of the Spaniards, the Inca Titu Cusi Yupanqui wrote his famous account of the conquest of the land of his forefathers by the Spanish crusaders. In describing the fateful scene in Cajamarca, when the Inca Atahualpa, then at the pinnacle of his power, was handed a Bible by Father Valverde, he calls the Holy Scriptures the *quilca* of the bearded ones. When he relates how the Spanish priest spoke silently with the white cloths, he means the white pages of the book. The writing in it is *quilca* to him. However, to the Inca, this kind of *quilca* was quite meaningless. His dignity as a deity affronted by the arrogance of the white men, he threw the book to the ground. This sacrilege is supposed to have been the cause of his being fired from a rusty Spanish cannon, sparking off one of the bloodiest of Christian massacres.

The Peruvians were probably not familiar with paper, unlike the Mayas and Aztecs, who made it from the fibers of a variety of ficus. This is probably why the Indian chronicler refers to white cloths and *quilca*, when he means the written pages of the holy book of the Conquistadors.

It is possible that certain designs which appear repeatedly on Inca garments were not mere decoration, but symbols of some significance, just like the images on some of the earlier textiles. More than eighty such symbols have been counted on Inca clothing. There are Peruvian scholars who regard them as a kind of hieroglyphic alphabet, and who even go so far as to assert that a kind of picture-writing existed in the Inca empire. Like the hieroglyphs of the Mayas, knowledge of them is supposed to have been restricted to the esoteric realm of priestly accomplishments. Banned by the Inca Pachacutic, the great reformer, they were forgotten. Pachacutic, it is said, was concerned only with glorifying the history of his own family, and was willing to condemn to oblivion all else belonging to an earlier age.

Every language on earth probably originated—as did Chinese, for example—in pictures of visible objects, which in the course of hundreds and thousands of years became ever more stylized until finally they were reduced to phonetic symbols. The fact that Incas used the word *quilca* to denote the Latin characters in the Bible, shows that they were instinctively aware of the original relationship between pictures and writing.

One of the most distinguished 16th century chroniclers, Sarmiento de Gamboa, mentions Inca wooden tablets that were kept in a hall of the Sun Temple at Cuzco. He states that the history of the Incas was portrayed in pictures on these wooden tablets. The same Sarmiento also describes painted cloths, on which ambassadors sent to various parts of the empire would make their reports to the great Emperor Pachacutic in pictorial form, similar to the practice of merchants sent to foreign parts by the Aztec rulers. But who can be certain that in the case of the Incas it was a genuine form of picture-writing, like that of the Mexicans, which exists in tribute lists, genealogies of princes, and in sacred folding books.

Many other chroniclers refer to picture and knotted records kept by the Peruvian elite as a way of noting historical events. The *quipu*—often confidently referred to as "knotted writing"—has by no means been fully interpreted yet, and still remains largely undeciphered. All that is known for certain is that the *quipu*, consisting of a number of knotted threads, was used for statistical purposes, including among other things the recording of stores of food, weapons and clothing kept in the state

warehouses. This much we know from reliable sources, but definitive evidence that they were used for recording astrological figures remains to be found. The few knot-records in the possession of museums today were all found in graves, and we have no exact details of these graves. It is quite possible that they were placed in the graves of administrative officials in much the same way that favorite weapons were placed in the graves of warriors, tools in those of artisans, and spindles and weaving instruments in women's graves. After the Spanish conquest, fanatical clergy destroyed as work of the devil all the *quipus* they could find so that, although the Spaniards may have deciphered them, there is no record of exactly how they were used.

The colors of the quipus found in graves are often faded. The colors identified whatever was being counted—population, animals, clothing, pots, weapons, metal—in brief, everything worth recording. Reading from top to bottom, the sequence of knots on each of the threads was equivalent in place value to the sequence of the individual figures in an Arabic number, read from left to right. Unlike other Indian cultures, which employed a system based on twenty, here the decimal system was used. So far no one has really proved that the knotted threads were also used as a mnemonic device for messengers' verbal reports and for the recitations of story-tellers. If this were so, here would be the beginnings of an abstract form of writing without recourse to pictures.

Less ambiguous evidence of the beginnings of a form of writing can be seen in certain symbols on rock drawings. A square with two intersecting diagonals may have meant "house," as it still does today for highland Indians, who use this symbol on a soft white stone as an amulet. There are no obvious parallels for symbols such as the concentric circles, crosses, wavy lines, spirals, rows of dots, horizontal and vertical lines, and many others found on rock drawings.

A more or less realistic image, or a complex or series of images may often form a complete sentence, but this cannot be compared with the far more developed rebus writing of the Aztecs.

Similar pictorial accounts occur in vase painting, and some of the images woven into fabrics, too, may well have been magic symbols.

A few of the Peruvian rock drawings may be quite old, although nowhere near so old as the French, Spanish and African cave paintings. A great many Peruvian rock drawings date only from Inca times, namely from the fifteenth century. This is evident from their style. Most Peruvian rock drawings consist of purely realistic images. As indicated earlier, a number of abbreviated symbols occur. These recur in different parts of the country, which implies that their meaning was probably constant.

Without the intervention of the Spaniards, some of the symbols which appear on vase paintings and textiles and which may be interpreted as the beginnings of a form of script writing, might perhaps have developed into true writing. This, however, is mere speculation. The fact is, that the representatives of the Church could read and write, and they exercised as much power as the Spanish administrative officials who were also literate (whereas the Spanish soldiers were for the most part illiterate). What incentive could the Peruvians have had to develop a script out of their own few symbols?

On the other hand, the theory put forward by one chronicler, that they once possessed a script which disappeared after royal suppression, is unlikely. There is equally little evidence to support the other theory of a major Peruvian collector, who claims that the beans painted on many of the Mochica vessels represent letters, because they contain incised symbols and often appear in connection with runners, who may well have been the bearers of written messages.

Record keeper with *quipu* presenting accounts to his master

Inca record keeper with *quipu* and calculating board

Many rock paintings quite simply tell a story, in more or less realistic images, like a picture-book. A man leads a llama with a lamb by a rope, followed by a male animal.

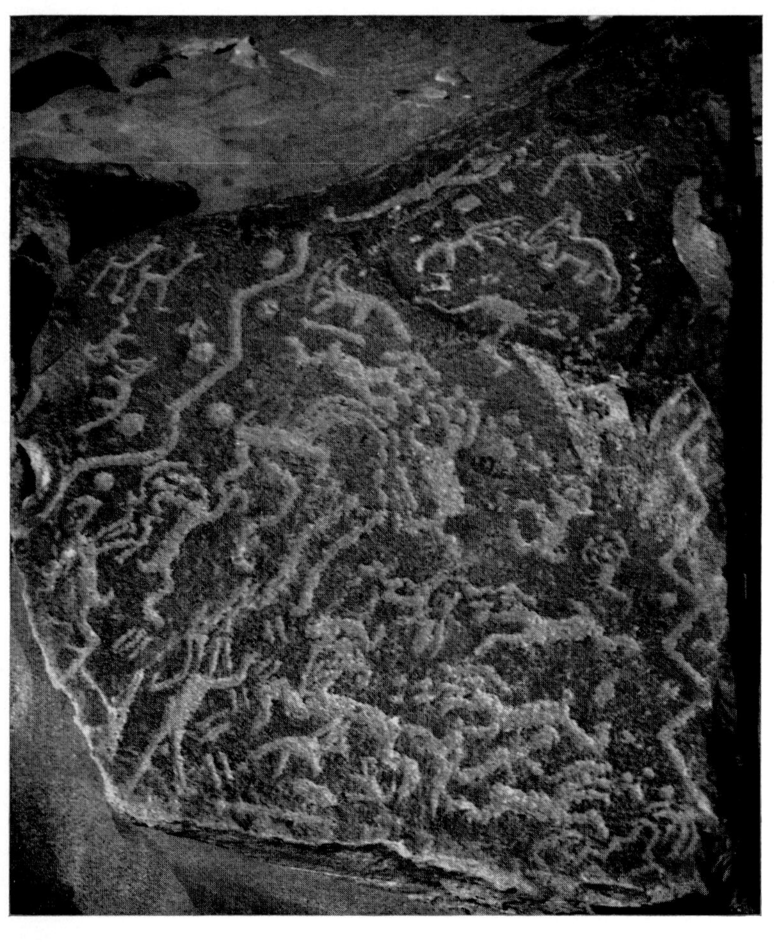

Facing page, above, left: zig-zag lines are one of the commonest symbols on the rock drawings in the Majes valley (south Peru). They have been interpreted as flashes of lightning, which along with thunderstorms bring the precious rain. The dancer in the upper part of the picture is probably invoking rain. The other symbols could stand for irrigation ditches.

Above, right: house symbols (squares with diagonals inside them) between the figures of various animals.

Below, left: this shows a dancer performing. Lightning flashes frame the picture. Below, right: the vertical and horizontal lines beside the masked dancing couple is sure to have had some special significance for the Peruvians of ancient times. The pictures are scratched onto volcanic boulders that lie scattered about in the desert region. Others are carved. Majes valley (south Peru).

Above: the course of a mythological event is worked into a cotton cloth in green and black threads. Fragment of an account of a myth unknown to us. The subject is combat. In the center of the fragment of cloth, a religious emblem towers up, as if in an enclosed temple area. Pachacamac (central Peru). Museum für Völkerkunde, Berlin.

Right: these signs and symbols come from a rock drawing east of the Andes, as indicated by their curious style.

Canoes with masked dancers. There is no doubt that the series of parallel, slanting lines were not merely ornamental, but had some definite symbolic meaning. On the left, at the bottom of the picture, animals leaping at each other, are pursued by a raging wild beast. Rock drawing in Toro Muerto. Majes valley (south Peru).

Chronological Table

Bibliography

Acknowledgements

Chronological Table

The Incipient Era	
Hunting, fishing and wild food gathering period	9000–4000 B.C.
Beginning of cultivation of beans, gourds, tubers, and capsicum pepper	4000–2500 B.C.
Cultivation of cotton and a small variety of corn	from 2500 B.C. onwards
Earliest ceramics	
A pre-ceramic period is succeeded by the cultivation of corn and the introduction of pottery, bringing the transition to the beginnings of a higher culture.	2500–1500 B.C.
Chavin Horizon	
Chavin religion and culture, spread over a wide area	1500 B.C. to 200 A.D.
Stone sculpture and fine ceramics	
Llama rearing	
Metal working, first identified only in Vicus	before the birth of Christ
Classical Era	0–800 A.D.
Apogée of regional cultures:	
Moche in the north	
Ancient Lima along the central coast	
Paracas-Nazcas in central southern Peru	
Flourishing of Tiahuanaco in the Bolivian highlands	about 500 A.D.
Post-Classical Era	800–1100 A.D.
Military and religious expansion of Tiahuanaco culture	
Flowering of urban centers and minor principalities	1100–1438
Historical Times	
Conquest of the Incas, beginning with Cuzco, the capital, in the southern highlands	from 1438
Inca Pachacutic Yupanqui	1438–1471
Inca Topa Yupanqui	1471–1493
Inca Huayna Capac	1493–1527
Division of the Inca Empire	1527
Inca Huáscar killed in Cuzco in 1532, by the generals of his brother, Atahualpa	1527–1532
Inca Atahualpa, regent in Quito, executed by the Spaniards in 1533	1527–1533
Beginning of the Spanish Conquest	1532

The earlier periods partially overlap. Preciser chronology begins with the use of radio carbon analyses. However, the results of this dating method have so far produced only a few more or less sporadic, unrelated dates.

Bibliography

Baudin, Louis, *So lebten die Inkas vor dem Untergang des Reiches.* Stuttgart 1957

Bennett and Bird, *Andean Culture History.* New York 1949

Bird, Junius, *Excavations in Northern Chile.* New York 1943

Bird, Junius, *Art and Life in Old Peru. An Exhibition.* New York 1962

Carrión Cachot, Rebeca, *Paracas Culture Elements.* Lima 1949

Carrión Cachot, Rebeca, *La mujer y el niño en el Antiguo Peru, in Inca, I.* Lima 1923

Cobo, Bernabé, *Historia del Nuevo Mundo (1653) 4 Vols.* Seville 1890–1895

Comas, Juan, *Principales aportaciones indígenas precolombinas a la cultura universal.* México 1957

Disselhoff, H. D., *Geschichte der Altamerikanischen Kulturen.* 2nd Ed. Munich 1966 (Also in Spanish and French translation)

Disselhoff, H. D., *Die Kunst der Andenländer,* in Kunst der Welt. Baden-Baden 1960

Disselhoff, H. D., *Neue Fundplätze peruanischer Felsbilder,* in Baessler-Archiv, Neue Folge III, Berlin 1955

Engel, Frédéric, *Sites et établissements sans céramique de la côte peruvienne,* in Journal de la Société des Américanistes, n. s. XLVI. Paris 1957

Engel, Frédéric, *Historia elmental del Peru Antiguo.* Lima 1965

Estrada, Emilio, *Las culturas antiguas del Ecuador en sus diversas épocas.* Guayaquil 1958

Garcilaso de la Vega, *Comentarios reales de los Incas (1609).* Buenos Aires 1943

Hissink, Karin, *Motive der Mochica-Keramik,* in Paideuma, V. Bamberg 1951

Horkheimer, Hans, *Nahrung und Nahrungsgewinn im vorspanischen Peru.* Berlin 1960

Horkheimer, Hans, *Zum heutigen Forschungsstand im mittleren Andenraum,* in Saeculum XIV, Freiburg/Munich 1963

Horkheimer, Hans, *Vicús.* Lima 1965

Kauffmann Doig, Federico, *Tres etapas pre-chavin.* Lima 1963

Krickeberg, Walter, *Amerika,* in Bernatziks großer Völkerkunde, III, Leipzig 1939

Krickeberg, Walter, *Felsbilder und Felsplastik bei den Kulturvölkern Altamerikas.* Berlin 1950

Kutscher, Gerdt, *Chimú. Eine altindianische Hochkultur.* Berlin 1950

Kutscher, Gerdt, *Nordperuanische Keramik.* Monumenta Americana I, Berlin 1959

Kutscher, Gerdt, *Sakrale Wettläufe bei den frühen Chimú.* Berlin 1960

Larco Hoyle, Rafael, *La escritura mochica sobre pallares,* in Revista Geográfica Americana, Buenos Aires 1943

Larco Hoyle, Rafael, *Escultura lítica del Perú Precolombino.* Lima

Linné, Sigvald, *Prehistoric Peruvian Painting,* in Ethnos, XVIII, Stockholm 1943

Lothrop, S. K., *Aboriginal navigation of the West Coast of South America,* in Journal of the Royal Anthropological Institute LXII, London 1932

Mason, Aldon J., *The Ancient Civilizations of Peru.* Pelikan Books. Harmondsworth 1957 (Also in German and Spanish translation)

Mejia Xesspe, Toribio, *Kausay. Alimentación de los Indios,* in Wira Kocha Vol. 1, Lima 1931

Montell, Gösta, *Dress and Ornament in Ancient Peru.* Göteborg 1928

Nordenskiöld, Erland, *The Copper and Bronze Ages in South America.* Göteborg 1929

Poma de Ayala, Guamán Phelipe (1584–1614), *El primer nueva corónica i buen gobierno.* La Paz 1944

Ravines, Rogger, *Investigaciones en el extremo Sur del Perú,* in Boletín del Museo Nacional de Antropología y Arqueología. No. 3. Lima 1965

Reiss, Wilhelm and Stübel, Alphons, *Das Totenfeld von Ancón in Peru. I–III.* Berlin 1880–1887

Rydén, Stig, *Archaeological Researches in the Highlands of Bolivia.* Göteborg 1947

Sarmiento de Gamboa, Pedro, *Geschichte des Inkareiches (1572).* Berlin 1906

Schmidt, Max, *Kunst und Kultur von Peru.* Berlin 1929

Seler, Eduard, *Die buntbemalten Gefäße von Nasca und die Hauptelemente ihrer Verzierung.* Gesammelte Abhandlungen, IV. Berlin 1923

Steward, Julian H. (Editor), *Handbook of South American Indians. II. The Andean Civilizations.* Washington 1946

Steward, Julian H. (Editor), *Handbook of South American Indians. V. The Comparative Ethnology of South American Indians.* Washington 1949

Tax, Sol (Editor), *The Civilizations of Ancient America.* Chicago 1951

Tello, Julio C., *Chavin, cultura matriz de la Civilización Andina.* Lima 1961

Trimborn, Hermann, *Das Alte Amerika.* Stuttgart 1959

Troll, Karl, *Die Stellung der indianischen Hochkulturen im Landschaftsaufbau der tropischen Anden,* in Ztschr. der Gesellschaft für Erdkunde. Berlin 1943

Ubbelohde-Doering, Heinrich, *Kunst im Reiche der Inka.* Tübingen 1952

Ubbelohde-Doering, Heinrich, *The Art of the Ancient Peru.* New York 1952

Uhle, Max, *Kultur und Industrie der südamerikanischen Völker. 2 Vols.* Berlin 1889–1890

Uhle, Max, *Pachacamac, Report of the William Pepper Peruvian Expedition of 1896.* Philadelphia 1903

Valcárcel, Luis E., *Historia de la Cultura Antigua del Perú. 2 Vols.* Lima 1943–1949

Weberbauer, Augusto, *El mundo vegetal de los Andes Peruanos.* Lima 1945

Willey, Gordon E., *Prehistoric Settlement Patterns in the Vicú Valley.* Washington 1943

Acknowledgments

All the plates were supplied by the author, and according to him, and to the best of the publisher's knowledge, the individual pictures were taken by the following photographers:

Anton, Ferdinand, Munich: Page 20 (right), 30 (left), 40 (below left), 50 (below), 55, 58 (above, two photos), 68 (above, left), 70 (left), 76, 81 (above), 99, 100, 104 (left), 105 (below, left-hand figure), 107 (right, above and below), 118 (above), 120 (above), 122 (above), 127, 135 (above), 138, 140 (above, left and center, and below, left and right).

Bräm, Zurich: Page 3, 39 (above left), 47 (center, right), 49 (above right), 56 (below, right), 58 (below, left), 59 (below, right), 102, 108 (below), 109 (above).

Braumüller, Munich: Page 18 (below), 19, 45, 52, 67 (above), 70 (right), 83, 110, 126, 139 (below, right).

Bredol-Lepper, Ann, Aachen: Page 22, 39 (below), 40 (above), 44, 57 (below), 60, 61 (above), 73, 77, 78 (below), 79 (above), 80 (below and center), 81 (below), 84, 85 (below), 94 (below), 107 (below, center), 117, 118 (below), 119, 120 (left), 123, 135 (below), 140 (above, right).

Casals: Page 139 (above).

Delange: Page 15.

Disselhoff, Hans Dietrich, Arequipa: Page 16 (above), 92 (center and below), 108 (above left), 131, 133 (below), 139 (below right), 142, 147, 150.

Guillen, Abraham: Page 17 (below), 29 (above right), 47 (below left), 66 (below left), 67 (below, right), 68 (right, center), 69 (below), 92 (above), 108 (above right).

Hamburgisches Museum für Völkerkunde, Photographic Section: Page 85 (above), 93 (below), 98 (below right), 103, 104 (above right), 107 (above, center), 125.

Hans Horkheimer: Page 28 (above left).

Linden Museum, Stuttgart: Page 16 (below), 20 (below), 35 (below right), 37, 39 (above, center), 46 (left, center), 50 (above left, and right), 96 (above), 98 (above left), 104 (below, right), 105 (below, right-hand figure), 106, 107 (below, left), 116 (below), 121 (below, left), 122 (left), 136 (above).

Matossi, E., Zurich: Page 40 (below).

Museum für Völkerkunde, Berlin *(Steinkopf, Walter,* Berlin): Dustcover, Page 17 (above, right, and left), 18 (above, left), 21 (above, left), 27, 29 (below, right), 30 (right), 33, 34 (below), 36, 38, 46 (above, and center, right), 49 (above, left, and below—2 photos), 50 (above, center), 51, 56 (above and below, center), 58 (below, right), 59 (left and above), 61 (below), 65, 66 (center), 67 (below, left), 68 (below), 69 (above), 71, 86, 91, 93, 116 (above), 121 (above and below right), 124, 137, 140 (below, center), 141, 149 (above).

Rojas, Ponce, Pedro, Lima: Page 46 (below), 58 (center).

Rautenstrauch-Joest Museum, Cologne: Page 21 (above right), 87.

Stadtbildstelle, Cologne: Page 21 (below, right).

Stucki, Hans: Page 29 (above, left).

Urteaga, Dr.: Page 66 (above).

Zevallos Menendez: Page 78 (above, left), 79 (below), 80 (above).

All the drawings in the text were taken from the following works, and redrawn by Frau Dr. Katharina Lommel:

Pages 9, 10, 23, 31, 64, 88, 111, 114, 146, taken from:
Travaux et mémoires de l'Institut d'Ethnologie XIII.
Felipe Guaman Pomo de Ayala
Nueva Corónica y Buen Gobierno
Codex péruvien illustré
Paris, Institut d'Ethnologie, 191 Rue Saint Jacques, 1936

Pages 12, 13, 14, 25, 26, 32, 43, 74, 112, 113, 144, 145 taken from:
Monumenta Americana, published by the Ibero-American Library, Berlin, editor G. Kutscher
Nordperuanische Keramik. Frühfigürlich verzierte Gefäße der Chimu. Gerdt Kutscher. Gebrüder Mann, Berlin, 1954.

Page 101 taken from:
Ferdinand Anton, Alt-Peru und seine Kunst, VEB E. A. Seemann Verlag, Leipzig, 1962.